Beyond the Diagnosis

No Labels, Just Lives

Cruz Elena Ibarra

ISBN: 979-8-9999752-4-9
Hablemos Editorial Project

To Elena and Alberto,

my little piece of heaven
and my little piece of life.

My driving force.
My reason.

You gave meaning
to every battle
and every dawn.

Prologue

This is not a book about medicine, laws, or diagnoses.
It is a book about what happens when life changes without warning, and a mother—or caregiver—is forced to learn a new language while her heart still struggles to understand.

Because before we can make sense of acronyms, processes, or prognoses, there is a deeply human experience that is almost never named: fear, confusion, guilt, exhaustion, loneliness...
and also that fierce love that appears when there are no manuals, and still, we must keep going.

This book was born to accompany that moment.

It does not seek to tell you what to do or how to do it "better."
It offers no formulas, quick solutions, or empty promises.
It offers something more honest and necessary: presence.
Words that give a name to what hurts. Spaces where there is no need to explain yourself or justify what you feel.

Because motherhood and caregiving, when intertwined with disability, are often lived in silence. Silence in the face of a society that still does not know how to embrace difference without reducing it to a label. Silence in the face of judgmental looks, words that wound without intention, and expectations that do not always reflect reality.

This book does not seek to break that silence with noise, but with companionship.

Here, there are no "cases" and no comparisons. Every story is different. Every process has its own rhythm. The journey of raising a child with a disability is not a competition, nor a measure of worth, nor a race that must be won.

What unites us is not the diagnosis.
It is love. The need to be seen.

The deep desire to offer our children a life that is dignified, respected, and full, in a world that still has much to learn about diversity.

This book is written from a place that is neither theoretical nor distant. It is written from the experience of walking this path from within: as a woman, as a mother, as a professional who has accompanied other families, and as someone who has learned that disability does not define a person, but it does profoundly transform those who love and care for them.

For a long time, we were taught to see disability as a personal tragedy—something that needed to be corrected or overcome. Yet Canadian activist Al Etmanski reminds us of something essential: disability is not the tragedy; the real tragedy is the way society treats people with disabilities.

This book is born precisely from the need to change that perspective: to stop seeing only a diagnosis and begin seeing the person—their dignity, their story, and their possibilities.

Throughout these pages, you will find real voices, reflections born from everyday life, emotional tools, and testimonies that do not seek to compete with one another, but to accompany one another. Because when a story is shared honestly, it no longer belongs only to the person who lived it —it begins to echo in the lives of others.

Beyond the Diagnosis is an invitation to see our children for what they truly are: people with worth, with rights, with soul. And to see ourselves with more compassion, less self-demand, and greater truth.

This book does not seek to close processes.
It seeks to open conversation, community, and awareness.
Because when we stop reducing life to labels and begin listening to whole stories, something changes—within us, and in the way we inhabit the world.
This is where that space begins..

Contents

1.

When the World Stands Still

"There are days when the world breaks in silence…
and still, the heart finds a way to keep beating."

The Impact of the Diagnosis and the First Fracture of the Soul

The day you receive a diagnosis for your child is something you never forget.

No matter how much time passes, that moment remains etched into you—like an open wound, and at the same time, like a mark that transforms you forever.

I remember the office, the doctor's words, the silence that weighed more than anything else.
I was listening, but I could not truly understand.
The technical phrases, the labels, the medical terms bounced through my mind as if they belonged to another language.

All I could feel was a knot in my throat, an overwhelming uncertainty, a cold heaviness in my chest, and the certainty that my life—and my child's life—would never be the same again.
It feels as though the world suddenly stops.

As if everything that once felt safe shatters into a thousand pieces.
You remain there, motionless, wondering if what you just heard is real, wishing you could wake up from a nightmare that does not end when you open your eyes.

Over time, I came to understand something no one had ever told me: that this feeling can return.
That life does not always shake us only once, and that even when we believe we have learned to live with uncertainty, it can suddenly place everything on pause all over again.

Every story has its own way of fracturing what once felt solid.
Then comes the silence.

The drive home with tears held back.
Your gaze lost beyond the car window, thinking about everything that will never be.

You arrive home, but it no longer feels like the same home.
It is the same door, the same walls… but you are no longer the same.
Something inside you has shifted, and you do not know how to place it back where it was.

No one prepares you for those moments.
No one teaches you how to hold the world together when it feels as though it is collapsing beneath your feet.

And meanwhile, the rest of the world continues moving as if nothing has happened.
People laugh, work, make plans…
and you feel suspended inside a painful pause that no one else seems to notice.

That is the moment when the world stands still.

And it is also—though it may take time to understand—the moment when a new path begins:
difficult,
uncertain,
filled with questions…
but sustained by a strength you do not yet know lives within you.

That is where a new mother is born.
A new woman.
One who, without ever having chosen this path,
will learn to live far beyond the diagnosis.

The Moment That Breaks Everything

There are moments that split life in two: the before and the after. A diagnosis is one of them.

They are words that, for the person speaking them, may simply be part of an everyday routine.
For you, however, they move through every part of your body and change everything.

The clock keeps ticking.
The doctor's voice continues speaking.
But none of it feels real.

Each term lands heavily, like a stone in your chest. You try to understand, but your mind clings to a single thought: this cannot be happening. There must be a mistake.

Denial often becomes the first refuge.

Believing that another opinion will change everything.
That tomorrow someone will say it is not as serious as it seemed.
That there has been some kind of misunderstanding.

And then, without warning, reality settles in.
Firm. Unyielding.

In that moment, many of the dreams you had quietly built begin to collapse. Not because you loved any less, but because the future you imagined no longer exists in the way you once knew it.

It does not matter whether the diagnosis comes at birth or years later: the impact is the same. Life changes abruptly, and what once felt certain begins to crack.

It is an invisible earthquake.
From the outside, sometimes no one notices.
But inside… everything fractures.

You may nod your head, ask questions, even smile out of habit. But within you, there is confusion, disbelief, and a fear so deep it becomes hard to breathe.

Because what hurts is not only the word itself, but what it represents:
a path you did not expect,
an unknown direction,
a life different from the one you had imagined for your child… and for yourself.

Suddenly, the future becomes blurred. You do not know where to begin or where to go. The famous "light at the end of the tunnel" is nowhere in sight yet. You are only taking the first step.

And in the middle of all this, I want to tell you something important: you are not alone.
That moment that breaks everything also opens a crack.

Perhaps you cannot see it yet, but little by little, light will begin to enter through it.
It will arrive in simple ways:
in a gaze that does not judge,
in a hand that holds yours,
in the voice of another mother who, with honesty and tenderness, will tell you: *I also felt like I could not do this… and I am still here.*

Because even if fear paralyzes you today and pain seems to cover everything, there is a strength within you that you do not yet know.

A strength born from the deepest kind of love.
That love will become your lighthouse.
It will hold you when you feel yourself falling.
It will guide you when you do not know what to do.
It will remind you that even if the path is different, it is still a path.

You do not need to have all the answers today.

You do not have to be strong all the time.

It is okay to cry.
It is okay to be afraid.
It is okay not to know.

What matters is to breathe.
To allow yourself to feel.
And to keep going, one step at a time.

There are other mothers here who understand.
Who do not judge.
Who walk beside you.

Because even though the moment that breaks everything hurts like nothing else…
it can also become the beginning of a different story.
A story with tears, yes,
but also with hope.

A story where love does not give up.

A story where you and your child remain at the center, even if the script has changed.

And in that story, dear mother, you are not alone.

The Echo of Silence

After a diagnosis, the right words almost never come.
And when they do, they rarely reach what is happening inside.

What comes first—almost always—is silence.

A strange, uncomfortable silence.
As if someone had lowered the volume of your life while everything around you continues to sound the same.

At first, it is an inner silence.
Because even you do not know what to say to yourself.

You are left without words, without a map, without a clear way to understand what is happening. Your heart moves faster than your thoughts, but nothing can catch up to it.

Then comes the silence of others.
A silence that hurts in a different way.
Among those closest to you, embraces become scarce and eye contact begins to fade. It is not always a lack of love. More often, it is fear.

Fear of saying the wrong thing, of hurting you more, of stepping into unfamiliar territory where there are no answers.
So they stay quiet.
They change the subject.
They talk about anything else.

It is not that they do not love you.
It is that they do not know how to accompany a pain that does not yet have a shape.

And you remain there, feeling small doors quietly closing around you, even though no one truly intended for that to happen.

That silence is not restful.
It does not soothe.
It becomes an emptiness that settles in your chest and echoes when the house grows quiet.

And then come the questions that burn:

What do I do now?
How am I supposed to move forward?
Who will understand this fear that even I cannot explain?

Meanwhile, the world outside continues.
People make plans, laugh, organize their lives.

And you find yourself living in a different kind of time, suspended between the before—which no longer exists—and the now, which you still do not know how to inhabit.
Psychologist Pauline Boss called this experience *ambiguous loss.*

A grief that is difficult to name because it is not about losing someone, but about watching the future we imagined begin to change.

Many families learn to live in that uncertain space while rebuilding a new form of hope.
That is where the need to speak begins to emerge.
To break the silence.
But speaking is not always easy.

Sometimes there are no words.
Sometimes it feels frightening to open your heart.

And many times, you do not know with whom you can do so without feeling judged or misunderstood.

Even so, every time you dare to share a small part of what you feel, the echo begins to soften.
And in its place, something new begins to appear: connection.

Connection with other mothers.
Connection with yourself.
Connection with the part of you that, though wounded, is still alive, still loving, still searching for light.

Little by little, you begin to discover that there are ears willing to listen, open hearts, hands that know how to hold without trying to fix anything.

Mothers who once felt silence as a wall—and learned to bring it down word by word, tear by tear.

You do not need to rush.
There is no correct way to move through this moment.
Each person finds her own rhythm.

The mothers you will meet along the way were once lost too. They do not carry magical solutions, but they hold something invaluable: understanding.

And that understanding arrives, embraces, and becomes a refuge.

Speaking will not always be easy.
Sometimes the words will tremble.
Other times they will not come at all.
And that is okay.

It is not about telling everything or explaining everything.
It is simply about allowing your truth, little by little, to have a place outside of you.

You do not have to speak to everyone.
You do not have to justify every detail.

You may choose with whom to share your story.

And when you do, something begins to change.
The echo softens.
The loneliness begins to crack open a little.

Voices appear that answer back, embraces arrive without being asked for, spaces emerge where your story is fully welcomed.

This book wants to be one of those spaces.

A place where silence is not a wall, but a doorway.

Where pain can be named without shame.
Where fear is understood.
Where hope—even if small—is allowed to stay.

Because beyond the diagnosis, life is still there.

Community is still there.
Love is still there.

And yes, there are words that heal.
And you deserve to hear them.

The World That Pulls Away

There is something almost no one tells you when a diagnosis arrives:

the world does not only change… sometimes, it also begins to move away from you.

Suddenly, you realize that life continues for everyone else with the same lightness as always, while you remain suspended in one place, trying to understand a reality no one else seems to notice.

What once felt natural—close friendships, spontaneous plans, long conversations—begins to feel distant.
As if you had crossed to another shore, and very few people were willing to take that step with you.

People who once felt very present begin to appear less and less.
Some step back gently, trying not to "intrude," as if solitude were something you needed.

Others keep their distance because this new path feels too big, too unfamiliar, too complex to walk closely beside you.
It is not always a lack of love.

Many times, it is uncertainty. A lack of understanding.
That quiet fear that appears when life changes the script and people no longer know how to move within a new story.

Invitations begin to fade.
Conversations become brief, careful, filled with phrases meant to comfort, but that never quite reach what you carry inside:
"Be strong."
"You can handle this."

"Everything will pass."
"Have faith."

Words spoken with good intentions,
but they never quite reach the exhaustion, the sleepless nights, the doubts,
or the weight of decisions that wake you in the middle of the night.

They do not reach that tight knot that forms as you try to hold yourself together, even while feeling shattered inside.

Some families begin to "avoid complications" and stop inviting you to gatherings, saying it is so your child will not become overwhelmed, without realizing that the excuse leaves you out too.

As if your child's difference were an inconvenience to their comfort.
As if your child's presence disrupted the fragile perfection of their routines.

And some friends, without meaning any harm, slowly adapt to a world where you no longer seem to fit.

Not because you have changed as a person,
but because your priorities now revolve around what matters most:

medical appointments,
evaluations, therapies, recommendations, hours spent searching…
anything that might represent hope for your child.
You have less free time, less energy, less room for light conversations.

And even though you are still yourself, many people no longer know how to find you in this new season of your life.
Little by little, without anyone saying it out loud, you begin to

remain in a separate place.

A place where you watch the world from the outside,
as if you had been moved into a parallel room where life unfolds at a different pace.

And then one of the quietest wounds begins to appear:
alongside your child, you also begin to be seen differently.
Your identity slowly begins to blur.

You stop being yourself,
and become "the mother of…"

You love your child deeply—that is never in question—
but it hurts to feel your own name becoming smaller.
To realize that almost no one asks how you are.
That distance hurts.
It hurts in the quietest part of the heart.

Not because you are searching for sympathy,
and not because you want the world to move at your pace.
It hurts because you long for genuine companionship.

Because carrying all of this alone is exhausting… deeply exhausting.
Because an honest word, a sincere presence,
can become profound relief when you feel as though you are rebuilding your life from the rubble.
And yes, sometimes the world pulls away.
It becomes smaller, quieter, more unfamiliar.

But within that same silence, something else begins to reveal itself:
the people who stay.

The ones who do not need long explanations.
The ones who do not run from exhaustion or unexpected tears.
The ones who do not try to rearrange your pain with quick words.
The ones who simply… remain.

Sometimes it is a friend who sits beside you without rushing.
Sometimes it is a neighbor who quietly leaves a meal at your door.
Sometimes it is another mother who looks at you and, without saying a word, makes you feel understood.

Within those small—but genuine—moments, a breath begins to return.
A space where you can be yourself without needing to justify anything.

A place where your child is not seen as a problem, but as a child who is loved and welcomed.
A bond that does not break after the diagnosis;
instead, it becomes stronger, more real.

Not everyone will stay.
And yes, that hurts.
But the ones who do stay… those are priceless.

With them, slowly and imperfectly,
you begin to rebuild a new world.

Perhaps smaller.
But also more authentic.
More honest.
More yours.

Between Fear and Guilt

When a diagnosis enters your life and settles into it,
it does not only change what you see—it also changes what you feel.

And that is when two shadows appear, becoming constant companions that are difficult to ignore in everyday life:

fear and guilt.

They both arrive without asking permission.
They sit beside you.
They follow you.
They breathe close to you.

Fear is immediate.
It does not give you time to process.

It is that sudden tightening in your chest when you try to imagine a future that now feels uncertain.

Fear of what is coming.
Fear of not knowing what will happen.
Fear of a path that seems harder than you ever imagined.
Fear of watching your child grow in a world that so often does not forgive difference.

Fear of not knowing whether there will be enough hands to help your child grow with dignity, with opportunities, with respect.

Fear of not always being able to be there.
Fear that love may not be enough to cover everything that is needed.

Fear of not having the strength, the patience, the resources, the knowledge…

In simple words:
fear of not being enough.

And how could you not feel it?

Many families walk through this same emotional storm when they receive a diagnosis.

Psychologist Robert Naseef, who has spent decades accompanying parents of children with disabilities, describes this moment as a profound mixture of love, fear, grief, and hope—all existing together within a parent's heart.

No one enters motherhood carrying a manual in her hands.
And certainly not this kind of motherhood, the one that forces you to make decisions you never imagined having to make.

You learn as you walk.
You guess, you ask, you improvise.
You hold your child with one hand while searching for answers with the other—answers that often seem impossible to reach.

There is no magic formula.
No clear instructions.
No absolute certainty.
There is only you, with your heart in your hands, trying to do the best you can.

Meanwhile, time does not stop.
Your child needs you now.
Their needs do not wait for you to figure out how to do everything

perfectly.

And here you are:
doing what you can…
and often, far more than you ever believed possible.

With fear, yes.
But also with love.

Guilt, on the other hand, is quieter.
It does not burst in all at once, but it weighs just the same.

It arrives slowly.
It hides in the corners of your thoughts.
It slips through the smallest cracks.
And before you realize it, it has settled into your mind disguised as questions that pierce the soul:

"Was it my fault?"
"Did I overlook some sign?"
"Did I do something wrong during my pregnancy?"
"Could I have prevented this?"
"What if I…?"
"If only I had…"

Questions without answers that dig in like thorns.

They are not born from logic.
They are born from wounded love.

And even when reason tells you they have no foundation,
your heart feels them as truths that scratch and ache.

You find yourself revisiting the past,
searching for causes where there are none,
because sometimes it hurts less to find someone to blame than to accept that there are things simply beyond your control.

And without meaning to, the outside world adds to that guilt.

Not always directly;
sometimes it arrives disguised as advice:

"Maybe what happened was…"
"Didn't they tell you…?"
"Perhaps if you had…"

And even when you know no one has walked in your shoes,
those words land exactly where it hurts most:
in the part of you that would give everything for your child,
and never wished for them to face obstacles.

Between fear and guilt,
one day you find yourself exhausted.
Trying to be strong when what you truly need
is, even if only for a moment,
not to have to be.

And that is where an essential truth begins to emerge—one you need in order to keep breathing:
You are not responsible for your child's condition.

No mother is.

Your love did not cause this.
Your body did not fail.
Your motherhood is not the root of something broken.

You did not arrive on this path from lack.

You arrived from love.

Being afraid does not mean you lack strength.
It means you continue moving forward even while trembling inside.
Doubt does not take away your worth.
Feeling tired does not make you incapable.
Fear is not weakness:
it is the measure of how deeply you love.

Guilt does not define you either.
It is only the reflection of the immense weight many mothers carry when they feel everything depends on them.
But not everything depends on you.
You do not have to carry the entire story on your shoulders.
You do not have to solve everything.

This path is not a test you pass or fail.
It is a constant learning process.
It is doing the best you can with what you have,
even when your heart trembles.

It is making mistakes and trying again.
It is crying in silence while still continuing to show up.
It is loving with everything you are, even when you feel something is missing.

And here is the truth that slowly begins to bloom:
You do not have to be perfect.
You do not have to know everything.
You do not have to carry everything.
Your child does not need a flawless mother.

Your child needs you.

With your doubts and your strengths.
With your fears and your relentless love.
With your presence, which becomes home even in the middle of chaos.

Accepting this does not happen overnight.
It arrives in small moments:
in every sleepless night,
in every achievement that fills your eyes with tears
and your heart with pride.

It arrives when you begin to understand
that guilt does not deserve the final word.
And that fear can walk beside you
without forcing you to stop.

Because what defines this journey is not fear.
Not mistakes.
Not doubt.

It is love.
That love that does not give up.

That love that keeps holding on even when you feel you cannot anymore.

That love that, even without knowing everything, is still willing to give everything.

And that, dear mother,
is more than enough.

Before We Continue…

The journey begins with a fracture, yes.

A precise moment—sometimes a minute, sometimes a single phrase—when everything you once believed was certain breaks without warning.

There is no sound beforehand to announce it.
No embrace to soften the fall.
There is only that diagnosis interrupting everyday life like a thunderclap that splits your story in two.

And then… silence.

A silence that is not calm, but disorientation.
A silence made of questions with nowhere to go,
of emotions colliding inside a chest that cannot hold them all.

That echo born within you also begins to be heard outside:
glances that do not know where to rest,
words that feel empty,
people who quietly step away without realizing the emptiness they leave behind.

In a matter of days—or minutes—you discover that it is not only your child who has been placed somewhere different…
you have too.
You are the same, and yet you are not.
The world keeps moving,
but you remain on a shore where everything feels slower,
more uncertain, more vulnerable.
Pain comes from many directions.

The news hurts.
The uncertainty hurts.

That vertigo of not knowing where to begin or where to walk next—it hurts.

It hurts to feel displaced, judged, or simply invisible.
It hurts to look in the mirror and not fully recognize the woman standing there:
tired, trying to understand a life that changed overnight.
And what hurts most
is the feeling that you have lost your name.

One day you were yourself—
with your story, your passions, your way of moving through the world— and the next, you wake up as "someone's mother."

A beautiful title, yes.

But also an overwhelming one when it seems to erase everything else.

Not because you do not love,
but because you still deserve to remain a person, a woman, a whole soul.
And yet, so often,
that personal space disappears beneath the demands of this new path.

To this deep pain, another persistent mixture is added:
fear and guilt.
Both settle in without asking whether there is room.

Fear arrives as an uncomfortable truth:

fear of failing, of falling short, of not protecting enough.
Fear of the future.
Fear of not being enough when all you want is to do everything perfectly.

Guilt—quieter, but just as sharp—
slips into your thoughts when you are alone.
It asks unfair, absurd, cruel questions.
And even when you know they are not true,
they still hurt.

And in the middle of this emotional storm—
between expectations, outside glances, and constant doubt—
a truth emerges that no mother wants to accept:

We were not prepared for this.
There is no map.
There is no training for holding together what is falling apart in your hands. And still… here we are.

Walking among invisible pieces.

Trying to rebuild a world that no longer feels steady.
Learning how to breathe through difficult decisions.
Holding our children's lives with a strength that,
many times, even we did not know we had.

This is the beginning.
Not a gentle or orderly beginning.
It is the start of a journey marked by disorientation,
vulnerability,
and emotional exhaustion.

But it is also—though at first it may be difficult to see—
the exact point where something new begins to grow within you.

A small strength, almost imperceptible.
Still without a name.
Difficult to explain.

But it is there:
in every deep breath,
in every glance toward your child,
in every clumsy and courageous attempt to keep going.

The kind that does not give up, even while trembling.
The kind that, little by little, will allow you to walk again.
Not because the path becomes easy,
but because the bond with your child
will teach you a different way of seeing, of holding, of living.
And even if you feel that the world has stopped and left you suspended in place, something within you has already begun to move:

a seed of resilience,
a spark of tenderness,
a quiet promise
that not everything is lost.

Because even in the middle of pain,
something begins to emerge— something that, one day,
will take your hand and help you keep going.

When the world stands still, something within us also begins to grow—
a strength still unseen, that one day will carry us forward again.

✦

2.

What Hurts in Silence

"What a mother keeps silent is not silence: it is a way of surviving while she finds the courage to speak."

The Invisible, the Unspoken, What No One Knows We Think

When my children's diagnoses arrived,
I believed the deepest pain had been that exact moment—
the moment I heard the words that divided my life
into a before and an after.

But over time, I came to understand that there was another kind of
pain, one much harder to explain.
One I never spoke out loud.

The kind that is neither shouted nor shared.
The kind you hide even from yourself.
The kind that appears in the middle of the night, when everyone is
asleep and you are still awake, your mind filled with questions
that have nowhere to rest.

A pain that disguises itself as strength
while you continue doing ordinary things:
cooking, driving, making appointments,
answering a phone call.

A pain with no witnesses.
Heavy like a stone
tied to your heart.

The kind that hides behind a smile,
behind a completed routine,
behind an "I'm fine" that truly means,
"I don't know how to keep going."

I did not share it with my family or my friends—
not even with the people closest to me.

It remained buried inside me
as though it were a shameful secret
that only I was supposed to carry.

Because I was afraid of seeming dramatic.
Or of someone thinking
I did not love my children enough.

I remember those nights when I would quietly get out of bed
because I could not sleep.
I walked through the house in silence,
careful not to wake anyone,
with a heavy heart
and the future reduced to a shapeless question.

Moments when I silently asked myself
whether I was doing things right,
whether my love would be enough
to cover everything my children needed.

Over time, I came to understand something essential:
sometimes what hurts the most
is not what happens outside,
but what remains within.
I discovered that the hardest part
is not always what the world says,
but what we keep repeating to ourselves:

the voice that demands,
the guilt that returns uninvited,
the exhaustion that hides
because "you have to be strong."

Over time, I understood that what wounds us most
is not always the diagnoses themselves,
but everything we silence after hearing them.

This chapter is born from that quiet place
where we so often keep the tears we never cry
and the thoughts we believe are too shameful to confess.

From that silence that does not make us stronger.
It only leaves us more alone.

Researcher Brené Brown has spent years studying human vulnerability, reminding us that showing ourselves as we truly are—with fear, doubt, and emotion—is also a form of courage.

Understanding, accepting, and sharing what we feel is one of the first steps toward lightening its weight.
That is why today I want to give voice to those silences.
To put into words
what we so often clench between our teeth.
Because speaking about what hurts
is not weakness:
it is an act of humanity.

There is no judgment here.
There are no expectations here.
There is companionship here.

A space to breathe.

And a deep desire
that no mother will ever again
have to remain alone
with what hurts her in silence.

What We Don't Dare to Say

There are thoughts that never leave our lips,
even though they live inside us every single day.

Thoughts that get stuck in our throats
because we were taught—from a very young age—
to silence what is uncomfortable, to hide what hurts,
to smile even when the soul is asking for a moment to breathe.

We do not say them for fear of being judged.

Because we believe there are emotions
a "good mother" should not feel.

Because we fear that, by naming them,
they will become heavier than they already are.

Or because it is difficult to accept
that we are human too.

That love can coexist with uncertainty.
That exhaustion is not always physical,
but deep and emotional.

These are the thoughts that return again and again,
like an uneasy whisper in the mind:

Will I be enough for my child?
Who will take care of them when I am no longer here?
Sometimes I feel so exhausted
I wish I could disappear for just a moment…
We keep these thoughts hidden in a corner no one sees—

alongside fear, doubt, exhaustion,
and that silent desperation
we do not always know how to explain.

We move through each day as best we can.
Taking care of what is urgent.
Doing what must be done.
Trying to remain calm
even while everything inside feels unsettled.

We continue through ordinary life
with an invisible knot inside us—
our minds somewhere else,
our hearts struggling not to collapse.

From the outside, everything seems normal.

No one imagines the conversation we carry within ourselves.
No one sees the questions tangled inside our chests.
People only see what we choose to show:

a calm expression,
a brief response,
a strength we have learned to wear.

But inside, we are holding ourselves together
however we can—
searching for strength in places
we never even knew existed.

Most of these thoughts
remain there, hidden.
And yet, the thoughts
we do not dare to say

do not make us bad mothers.

They make us real mothers.
Women who feel.
Who doubt.
Who sometimes need a moment just to breathe.

Women who love their children deeply
and still long for a little lightness.

Women who continue moving forward
even when the body asks for rest
and the heart asks for help.

Because love is not always visible.
It is not always celebrated.

Sometimes it appears
in an attentive glance,
in a sleepless night,
in a medical appointment
that no one else attends.

Sometimes it disguises itself as patience
when there is no energy left.

Sometimes it is held together by invisible threads,
but it remains there— steady, stubborn, real.
Sometimes it lives in the embrace we give
even when we are about to break inside.

Giving voice to these thoughts
does not make them darker.

Quite the opposite.

When we name them,
when we dare to share them,
we discover something essential:
we are not alone.

So many other mothers think the same.
Feel the same.
Remain silent about the same things.

And then, the silence begins to break.
And through that crack, a little relief begins to enter.

A soft breeze that reminds us
we are not wrong for feeling.
We are not failing for doubting.
We are not broken for growing tired.

We are alive.
We are learning.
We are loving without manuals and without guarantees.

And that—though it is rarely spoken about—
is a profound act of courage.
An act of love,
not only toward our children,
but toward ourselves
and toward those who, without even realizing it,
need to hear these words
to feel a little less alone.

The Exhaustion No One Sees

Exhaustion is too small a word
to describe what we live through.

Because it is not only about being tired
from daily routines.
It is a weariness that settles
into every corner of the body,
the mind,
and the soul.

An exhaustion that is not measured in hours of sleep,
but in the number of times
we have held the world together
without anyone noticing.

Physical exhaustion, of course,
is the most visible.
The exhaustion of running from one medical appointment to another.
Of waiting endless hours in silent hallways.
Of fitting therapies into the schedule,
cooking, cleaning, caring for other children,
meeting work responsibilities,
trying to care for a relationship.

That exhaustion is felt in the bones,
in the back,
in the legs.
And sometimes, if you are lucky,
it softens a little— with a nap,
with a day of rest, with someone reaching out a hand.

But there is another kind of exhaustion.
A deeper one.
A quieter one.

The kind almost no one sees—
and the kind that hurts the most.

Emotional exhaustion.
Mental exhaustion.

The kind that does not disappear
after eight hours of sleep
or a long weekend.
It is the weariness of carrying a mind
that is always on.

Of thinking about a thousand things at once.
Of never being able to fully let go.

It is living in a constant state of alert.
Anticipating what your child may need.
Imagining what could happen.
Preparing yourself to respond if something goes wrong.

It is feeling that you cannot truly relax
because there is too much at stake.
It is carrying an uncertain future.
Questions that never end.

The weight of protecting your family
in a world that does not always understand.
It is, simply, never being able to disconnect.
This exhaustion is silent.
From the outside, people may see you smiling,

functioning, getting through the day.

Few know what is happening inside:
a mind that never turns off, even at night,
a heart beating with anxiety
even when everything appears fine,
tears that sometimes appear
without even knowing why.

It is the feeling of standing at the edge
and still continuing forward
because there is no other choice.
The exhaustion no one sees
is, in truth, a cry of the soul.

A reminder that we are not machines.
That love, too, caries weight.

Psychologist Charles Figley, who has spent years studying the emotional impact of long-term caregiving, described this experience as compassion fatigue: a deep exhaustion that emerges when love and responsibility keep us in a constant state of alert for someone else's well-being.

Many mothers live with it
without even knowing it has a name.

It is not weakness.
It is the human cost of caring deeply.
The cost of strength itself.
And we are paying it
with our bodies,
with our hearts,

with our silence.

Naming this exhaustion
does not make it disappear.
But it does something important:
it reminds us
that we are not alone.
That we are not the only ones.

That there are other mothers
feeling the same,
carrying the same,
silencing the same.

Admitting it does not make us less strong.
It makes us human.
Human beings who grow tired.
Who doubt.
Who remain standing
even when everything inside
is asking for rest.

And within that shared humanity,
within that truth finally spoken out loud,
a little light begins to enter.
The light of knowing we are accompanied.
The light of understanding
that we do not have to carry everything alone.

The light of recognizing
that the love we give—
even through exhaustion—
is still immense.

The Mask of Strength

And there we go…
moving forward as best we can,
learning to live in a reality
no one ever taught us how to inhabit.

Over time—almost without realizing it—
we begin to wear a mask.

One that smiles at gatherings.
One that says "I'm fine"
when inside, we are not.

One that gives the impression
that we have everything under control,
even when, many times,
we are barely holding ourselves together.

We do not wear it out of falseness.

We show strength
because we believe it is what is expected of us.
Because we were taught that being a mother
means enduring, resisting, holding everything together.

That a mother must be tireless,
unbreakable,
capable of carrying everything
without pause, without doubt, without tears.

We learned that showing exhaustion means failing.
That crying is weakness.

That asking for help makes people uncomfortable.

And so, little by little,
we put on this mask
that tries to protect us,
while inside,
a silent battle is unfolding.

A mask that says:
"everything is under control,"
when in reality
we are surviving moment by moment,
doing the best we can with what we have.

That mask is heavy.

Heavy on the chest.
Heavy on the back.
Heavy on the soul.

Every time we say "I can handle it"
when we can no longer keep going,
something inside us shrinks a little.

Not because we want to deceive the world,
but because we are trying to survive.

Sometimes we even learn to cry in the shower,
where the water carries our tears away and leaves no witnesses
behind.

We protect ourselves from hurtful comments,
from pitying looks, from unfair comparisons,
from advice that does not understand

the complexity of our daily lives.

We protect ourselves from that
"if I were in your place…"
that falls like a stone
onto a burden already too heavy.

But in trying to protect ourselves,
we lose something valuable:
the possibility of showing ourselves as we truly are.

Women who love deeply.
Who doubt.
Who grow tired.
Who also need support.

Being strong is not staying silent.
It is not pretending.
It is not carrying everything alone.

Being strong, on this path,
means daring to be vulnerable
and still remain standing.

It is being able to say "I can't do this anymore"
without feeling ashamed.
It is allowing someone to see
what we truly carry inside.

Breaking the mask is not easy.
Sometimes it takes time.
Sometimes, years.
But when we do—

even if it is only in front of one person
who knows how to listen without judgment—
something softens.

At first, it hurts.
It feels like shedding
a skin we wore for far too long.

But then… the air begins to come in.
And we remember that we, too, deserve
rest, comfort, a space where we do not have to prove anything.

Because being strong is not denying pain.

Being strong is continuing to love
even when the path feels heavy.
It is allowing yourself to feel,
to cry,
to ask for help,
to breathe.

It is remaining standing, yes…
but as yourself.
Whole.
Human.
Without masks.

That is the kind of strength that truly sustains:

the kind born from truth
and grounded in love,
not in appearances.

You Are Not Failing

There are days when an inner voice begins to plant doubt.

Days when you ask yourself if you are doing enough,
if you are responding the right way,
if you are failing at something you cannot even name.

You look at yourself from the outside
and judge yourself harshly.

Because you cry.
Because you grow tired.
Because sometimes you do not know what to do.
Because there are moments when fear takes over
or the silence feels too heavy.

And then that dangerous idea appears—
quiet, persistent:

"Maybe I'm not as strong as I should be."

But let me tell you something,
clearly and with respect:

You are not failing.
You are not failing for feeling exhausted.
You are not failing for doubting.
You are not failing for needing a pause.
You are not failing for grieving the life
you once imagined.

None of that makes you less of a mother.

None of that diminishes your love.
You are living something no one teaches you how to live.
Carrying a responsibility
that cannot be measured in words.

Loving in a way
that transforms you, wears you down,
and asks more of you
than you are often able to give.

And still, you continue.
With fear,
with exhaustion,
with questions…
still, you continue.

That is not failure.
That is endurance.
That is love.

Failure would be surrendering to indifference.
To stop seeing.
To stop trying to understand.

And you are still here.
Holding on.
Learning.

Sometimes surviving, yes.
But always present.

You are not failing
because you do not have all the answers.
No one does.

You are not failing
because you cannot do everything.

No one can.

You are doing what all real love does:
the best you can,
with what you have,
in the middle of what hurts.

And that—
even when it does not always feel like enough—
is enough.

Breathe.

Not so you can keep running,
but so you can remember
that you matter too.

You are not failing.
You are living something difficult…
and you are walking through it
with an open heart.

Before We Continue…

What hurts in silence cannot be seen from the outside.
It does not appear in family photos
or in hallway conversations.
It is not visible in the smile we offer when we arrive at a gathering,
nor in the "I'm fine" we repeat out of habit.

It hides in the thoughts we do not dare to speak aloud,
in the exhaustion no one imagines,
in the loneliness we feel even when we are surrounded by others,
in that mask of strength
we learned to wear so we would not make anyone uncomfortable.

It is a pain that goes beyond diagnoses.
It is the weight of living in constant alert,
of holding everything together without rest,
of carrying fears and guilt
that do not always have a name.

It is the difficulty of letting our guard down,
of allowing ourselves to be fragile
without feeling as though we are failing.

And still, we continue.
We continue loving.
We continue caring.
We continue organizing, supporting, figuring things out.

We continue giving the best of ourselves,
even when it feels as though there is nothing left.
Many times, we continue in silence.
Because we fear being judged.

Because we believe that a "good mother"
should not grow tired, or doubt,
or need help.

But there is something that needs to be said clearly, without hesitation:

Feeling all of this is not failing.
Growing tired is not failing.
Doubting is not failing.
Needing a moment to breathe is not failing.

What hurts does not make us weak.
It makes us human.

That is why this chapter exists.

To give a name to the invisible.
To say out loud
what we have so often kept silent:
that we are tired,
that we are afraid,
that sometimes we do not know how to keep going.

And yet, we are still here.

When we break the silence—even if only a little—
we discover something essential:
we are not alone.

That other mothers have felt the same.
That what we once believed was a flaw
is, in truth, a shared experience.

Vulnerability does not diminish our worth.
It connects us.
It humanizes us.
It gives us back permission to be real.

Naming what hurts
does not change our children's reality,
but it does transform the way we live within it.

Because it stops being a solitary burden
and slowly begins to become
a path walked together.

And little by little, something begins to settle inside us:
silence becomes companionship,
guilt loosens its grip,
exhaustion finds a small breath of relief.

The mask falls.
Not to reveal us as broken,
but as true.

And from there—from that truth—
it becomes possible to keep going.

Not out of obligation,
but with greater clarity,
with more compassion toward ourselves,
and with the certainty
that we are not failing.

"What we keep silent in solitude, once shared,
becomes strength."

3.

Wounds That Go Unnamed

*"The soul's wounds do not ask for explanations;
they ask for companionship, so they do not feel so alone."*

Between Uncertainty and the Need to Feel Accompanied

If in the previous chapter we looked inward—
toward silence, exhaustion, and the emotions we learned to hide—
here, we begin to look around us.

Because not all wounds are born within us.

There are wounds that do not bleed,
and yet they hurt just the same.

Wounds that do not appear in any test
or show up on an X-ray,
because they do not live in the body…
they live in the soul.

They are deep marks that begin to form
when a mother understands
that her child's life will not follow
the path she once imagined.

They are not wounds born from a single moment.
They do not come only from the diagnosis
or from the emotions we keep in silence.

These are wounds born outside of us.
They are born in a world that was not built for our children.
In systems that fail.

In doors that close without explanation.
In decisions that leave us standing at the margins.
They are wounds that open little by little,
sometimes without anyone noticing.

In every medical appointment where we feel ignored.
In every comment that minimizes what we live through.
In every waiting room where it hurts to feel invisible.

In every careless phrase that lands
exactly where it hurts the most.
In every moment we realize
our family no longer quite fits in.

These are wounds that accumulate over time.
They appear when we walk into a school
and are met with distrust.

When a specialist minimizes
what we witness every single day.
When we feel we must prove,
again and again,
that our child deserves the same opportunities
as any other child.

They open when policies,
paperwork, waiting lists,
and endless processes
seem to say—without saying it:
"this was not designed for you."

When society expects "normality"
and does not know what to do with difference.

Sociologist Erving Goffman called this process stigma—
the quiet way a society distances or marginalizes
those who do not fit its norms.
Invisible barriers that end up deeply affecting

the lives of those who live close to difference every day.

When a look makes us feel out of place.
When a comment reveals ignorance,
fear, or even rejection.

When we realize that what feels simple for other mothers—
a trip to the park, a birthday party,
a school meeting—
for us requires preparation, courage,
fear, and often,
the possibility of facing other people's discomfort.

These are the wounds that are not always named.

Because few people truly understand
what it means to care, to protect,
and to fight every single day.

Because there are feelings we believe are forbidden:
insecurity, anger, frustration.
And yet, we have all felt them.

These are wounds we learn to carry
while handling what is urgent,
while searching for therapies,
while fighting for services,
while trying to make sure
our children are seen, heard, and respected.

Wounds born in that in-between space
between what we wish for our children
and what reality allows.
They hurt because they should not exist.

And yet, they do.
And even if we do not always say it,
these experiences leave marks:

the tension of always being alert,
the feeling of having to fight for basic things,
the emotional exhaustion of constantly asking,
explaining,
clarifying,
justifying.

This is where this chapter comes from.
From those wounds that do not only live within us,
but emerge
when everyday life confronts us
with a world that is still not prepared
to truly welcome our children.

Wounds that speak of injustice,
of barriers,
of a lack of empathy
in places where it should already exist.
Here, we are going to name them.
Not from complaint,
but from truth.
From the need to recognize
that what we face
is not only personal,
but also social,
structural,
and cultural.

And that understanding these wounds—

understanding where they come from—
helps us release
the guilt that does not belong to us.

Because we are not alone in this.

Because these wounds
are shared by thousands of mothers
who, like you and like me,
have had to become advocates, interpreters,
mediators, and bridges
between our children
and a world that is still learning how to include.

This chapter is a space
to look at them directly.

To understand them.
To remember that they are not your failures,
but failures of the system.

And from there,
to begin finding strength—
not from pressure,
but from awareness—
to keep building paths
that are more just,
and more human.

Not only for our children,
but also
for the children of others.

Learning to Walk Without Certainty

Uncertainty becomes a constant presence
in our lives from the moment we are told
that our children's lives will follow a different path.

It does not disappear with time.
It does not completely fade.
It simply changes shape,
moves alongside us,
and settles into everyday life.

There is no manual that tells us what to expect tomorrow.
There is no calendar marking when
the progress we long for with all our hearts will arrive.

There are no certainties to hold onto
when we try to imagine the future.

Each family moves forward as best they can,
lighting the path with small moments of hope,
celebrating steps that others might not even notice,
feeling a knot in the throat
over things others would never fear.

And yes…
that uncertainty is heavy.

It is heavy because we wish we could guarantee them
a life that is fair, loving, and respectful.
It is heavy because we want to protect them
from everything the world still does not understand.
And because, even when we fight with all our strength,

we know we cannot control every step that lies ahead.

We want the world to welcome them with respect.
But we have no guarantees that it will.

And still, we continue.
Uncertainty, however,
also transforms us.

It forces us—sometimes against our will—
to see the present differently.
To value the small victories
that, within us,
feel enormous.

That new sound
that took weeks of practice.
That word spoken with effort.
That gesture that seems simple,
but requires more coordination than anyone could imagine.

That unexpected step.
That smile that arrives without warning
and somehow has the power
to mend an entire day.

That day without a crisis.
That night without staying awake.
All of this reminds us that every achievement,
no matter how small it may seem from the outside,
becomes immense when seen through love.

Every step forward carries within it
a much larger story—

a story of repetition,
of patience,
of accumulated minutes,
of tireless love.

And when we begin to see it this way,
we understand something important:
our children are not moving slowly.

They are moving at their own pace,
with extraordinary strength.
In the midst of so much uncertainty,
what we need most
is not empty compassion.

Nor phrases
that try to minimize
or soften what is difficult.
What we need
is real support.

Support that takes shape in
prepared schools,
professionals who truly listen,
doctors who guide without rushing,
spaces where our children
are seen with dignity,
not with pity.

Because they are not "poor things."
They are not "sick children."
They are whole human beings,
with their own unique way

of learning, communicating, moving, feeling,
and being in the world.

No more and no less than any other child.

Our children deserve respect.
They deserve services
that truly respond to their needs.

They deserve genuine opportunities,
not favors.

And we, as mothers,
deserve to stop walking through shadows.

We deserve environments that support us,
that understand us,
that hold us up.

Because uncertainty becomes more bearable
when it is not lived in solitude,
when hands reach toward us
instead of doors closing.
Uncertainty will still be there, yes.
But not as a weight that crushes us,
rather as part of the path
we learn to walk
with greater awareness,
with community.

And with the immense love that sustains us every day,
even in a world
that is still learning
how to do better.

When Words Hurt More Than Diagnoses

There are words that pierce the soul.
They do not appear in medical records
or in clinical reports,
yet they leave deeper marks
than anything printed on paper.

They are phrases spoken without thinking,
thrown carelessly as though they carried no weight,
yet they land exactly where
a mother's heart is most vulnerable.

Sometimes they come in a "sympathetic" tone,
other times disguised as advice,
and sometimes with a bluntness
that hurts far more than it helps:

"Poor thing… how sad."
"Poor you, you must be suffering so much."
"Maybe you're exaggerating… he seems perfectly normal."
"That's just a lack of discipline."
"Why send him to school? He's only going to suffer there."
"If he were my child, I would do things differently."

Each of these phrases
is a door quietly closing.

A reminder that many people
still do not know how to look at difference
without fear,
without judgment.

Without that veil of incomplete ideas
that reduces our children
to a distorted version
of who they truly are.

What hurts is not only the word itself,
but everything behind it:

the heavy glance,
the distrust,
the lack of empathy,
the ignorance that is not always ill-intentioned,
but still wounds just the same.

It hurts because it reveals
how little people understand about our children's lives
beyond the labels.

How little they know
about the daily effort our children make
to adapt,
to fit in,
to regulate themselves,
to endure.

Especially when the disability is not visible,
when "it doesn't show,"
when the world assumes that
if it cannot be seen,
then it does not exist.

And there we are…
performing emotional balancing acts:
explaining what should be obvious,

defending what should never have to be defended,
holding with our own hands
the dignity of our children.

Because we know the world
still does not know how to do that—
at least, not often enough.
Because our children
do not need pity.

They do not need to be seen
as tragic, fragile, or incomplete.
Nor do they need to be romanticized
as "inspirational"
simply for existing.

What they need is not empty compassion,
but open paths.
Spaces where they can participate
without being questioned,
without having to prove again and again
that they deserve to be there.

They need people willing
to approach with curiosity and respect,
not fear.
Professionals who know how to see
their abilities before their challenges.
Communities that understand
that diversity is not a threat,
but a natural part of shared life.

When other people say

those hurtful things,
they do not hurt because of us.

They hurt because they touch directly
the people we love most.

Because they remind us that,
instead of finding allies,
we often encounter barriers
built from misunderstanding.

Because they reveal how far we still are—
not only from the inclusion so often spoken about,
but from a genuine understanding
of what it means
to live disability from within.

Not from fear.
Not from prejudice.
Not from simplified ideas
that fail to hold the complexity of real lives.

That is why speaking matters.

Naming what those words cause matters.
Not to fight everyone.
Not to point fingers.
But to create awareness.
To plant questions
where there was once only judgment.
To gently correct—when there is openness—
without raising our voices.

To set boundaries without losing calm.

To defend dignity
without losing humanity.

Perhaps one day
we will stop hearing phrases
that reduce,
invalidate,
and wound.

And begin to hear
what should have been said
from the very beginning:

"Your child matters."
"Your child contributes."
"Your child deserves to be here."
"What your child brings into the world is valuable."

Because that is the truth.

And even if not everyone is able to see it yet,
it still deserves to be spoken,
upheld,
and defended with love.

The Judgment in Others' Eyes

Sometimes, words are not needed for us to feel hurt.

There are reactions that wound
without a single phrase being spoken.

A look is enough.

Mothers of children with disabilities know this well.

Sometimes it is enough to walk into a store,
arrive at a park, sit in a restaurant,
or enter a party
to notice how the atmosphere shifts the moment we appear.

Eyes linger a second longer than usual.
Some people try to hide it.
Others do not.

But we feel it.
We read it.
We recognize it.

It is that look that tightens
when your child makes an unexpected movement.

The one that fixes itself on them
when they speak louder than expected
or do not respond the way they "should."

The look that silently asks:
"What's wrong with this child?"

The one that, without saying a word, reproaches:
"Do something."
"Control them."
"Don't let them act like that."

These are looks that do not seek to understand,
but to classify,
to judge.

Looks that reduce your child
to a behavior,
to a difference,
to a label.

Looks that do not see the story behind them.

They do not see the effort,
the therapies,
the patience,
the immense courage
within every one of their actions.

That silent judgment is exhausting.

It forces us to remain constantly alert,
as though we must anticipate every reaction
so we do not make others uncomfortable.

It makes us feel
that we must explain,
justify,
soften,
translate our children to the world.

And sometimes, without even meaning to,
it leaves us with the unfair feeling
that we are "bothering" others
simply by being there.

It should not be this way.

Our children are not a spectacle.
They are not something to observe from a distance.
They are not a flaw
in someone else's idea of a perfect world.

They are people.
Children, teenagers, young adults, adults.

With feelings, preferences, fears, joys,
and their own ways of being in the world.

They have the right to make noise,
to laugh,
to ask questions,
to move differently,
to take up space
without being examined
as though someone must decide
whether they "deserve" to be there.

Raising a child with a disability
in a world that was not designed for them
means anticipating those looks
and trying to protect them from a society
that still does not understand neurodiversity.

As mothers,

those looks hurt us, yes…
but they also awaken us.

They remind us that there is still much to be done.

That the world needs to learn,
to listen,
to change the way it looks at
what it does not understand.

We will not always have the strength to explain.
We will not always feel emotionally able
to educate everyone who looks at us strangely.

And that is okay too.

We are not obligated
to give explanations every time we leave the house.

But there will be days—
and those days matter—
when instead of lowering our gaze,
we will hold it calmly.

Days when we will respond
with a simple word,
with a steady smile,
with a phrase that gently puts things back in place:

"He is who he is, and that's okay."
"She has the right to be here,
just like anyone else."
Sometimes transformation begins there:

by not hiding,
by staying,
by refusing to withdraw from spaces
that belong to us too.

May the day come
when those eyes
no longer look with judgment,
but with respect.

When a gesture of discomfort
becomes
a gesture of welcome.

When instead of asking,
"What's wrong with them?"
someone comes closer and says:
"What's their name?"
"What do they like?"

That will be the day
when society begins to see
what we already know:

that difference
is not something broken that needs fixing,
but part of the profound richness
of being human.

Because empathy is inclusion too.

The Wound of Having to Explain, Over and Over

Being the mother of a child with a disability
often means living with a script
we never asked to learn.

A script that repeats itself on our lips
more times than we would like,
as though the world needed justification
to accept our children's existence.

We explain things at school,
so they can understand
that learning differently is still learning.

We explain things during medical appointments where, ironically,
we should find guidance,
not disbelief.

We explain things at family gatherings,
when someone asks—
with more curiosity than sensitivity—
"but… what do they have?"

And we even explain ourselves to strangers:

in the grocery line,
at the park,
in a restaurant,
when a lingering look turns into questioning
disguised as interest.

And of course, it should not be this way.

We should not feel obligated to translate
our children's lives
so others can "understand" them—
or worse,
approve of them.

We should not carry the responsibility
of proving, again and again,
that what is different also belongs,
is equally valid,
and has a place in the world.

The wound of always having to explain
is not only exhaustion.

It is the constant feeling of defending
something that should be obvious:

that our children deserve to be exactly where they are.

That they have the right to exist in this world
without anyone questioning their presence.

That we should not have to ask permission
to take up spaces that belong to all of us.

Every explanation hurts because of what it reveals underneath:

the lack of understanding,
the absence of empathy,
the habit of seeing difference
as a problem to fix
or a mystery someone feels entitled to solve.
But it also hurts because, many times,

we feel forced to choose
between two equally unfair paths:

to remain silent
and endure the discomfort,
or to open up our children's lives
to satisfy a curiosity
that does not always come from respect.

Having to explain ourselves all the time is exhausting.

It drains emotional energy.
It makes us feel as though we must justify
what needs no defense.

And it places on our shoulders a weight
that, in truth,
does not belong to us alone.

Because society still has much to learn.

It must learn to look without judging.

To respect without demanding details.
To coexist without asking for explanations.

It must learn
that not all disabilities are visible.

That not all differences can be noticed at first glance.

And that none of them—
visible or invisible—

should be placed under public scrutiny.

We should not have to give improvised lessons
in humanity
with every step we take.

We should not have to be
the constant defenders
of what is fundamentally human.

We should not feel
that we are "interrupting normality"
simply by entering a shared space
with our children.

What we truly need
is not to repeat more explanations,
but to find places where they are no longer necessary.

Places where our children
are seen with respect,
not curiosity.

Where we can simply exist—
without justifying,
without clarifying,
without translating their existence
so others can understand it.

Until that day comes,
we will keep speaking, yes.
But not only explaining:
we will keep educating,

when there is openness.

Opening paths,
challenging old ways of seeing,
teaching through example.

Even when we do not always have the strength
or the desire to do so.

Because every time we respond with dignity—
even when it hurts inside—
we plant a seed.

Sometimes it grows.
Sometimes it does not.

But one day, together,
we will grow an entire forest.

And perhaps then,
at last,
we will be able to walk beside our children
without feeling the need to explain anything at all.

Because the world
will finally have learned
something so simple,
and so urgent:
that our humanity
does not require explanation.

Before We Continue...

The wounds that go unnamed are, almost always, the ones that weigh the most.

They have no medical code and do not appear in any report,
yet they live within the everyday reality we walk through alongside our children.

They are the small cracks that form
from words that should never have been said,
from looks that make us uncomfortable,
from silences that hurt,
from explanations we should never have to give.

They are invisible wounds, but constant ones.

They live in the uncertainty of not knowing
how far the world's understanding will reach.
In the weight of always being alert.

In the exhaustion of defending what should be obvious.
In the quiet sadness of living in a society
that still does not understand diversity as part of its richness.

And yet, these wounds—though painful—also awaken something within us.

They push us to look beyond the personal
and recognize that not everything we carry is born within.

That there is much that still needs to change outside of us:
in systems, in perspectives,

in the ways people learn to live alongside one another.

Our children do not need pity
or phrases disguised as compassion.

They do not need to be "explained" in order to be accepted.
They do not need to be defended in order to belong.

They need something far simpler and far deeper:
to be recognized as whole human beings.

To be seen for who they are, not through the lens of a label.

To be supported by a society
that understands diversity is not a flaw,
but another expression of what it means to be human.

And we, as mothers, walk with these wounds, yes…
but we also learn—sometimes without even realizing it—
to transform them into clarity, into awareness,
into voice.

We do not speak to justify.
We speak to open paths.

We do not explain to convince.
We explain—when there is openness—
to plant respect.

We do not raise our voices to fight,
but to remind the world of something too often forgotten:

that our children deserve dignity,

real opportunities,
and a rightful place in the world.

This chapter is a reminder
of the silent wounds we carry,
but also of the strength that emerges when we stop hiding them.

Because when the invisible is named,
it no longer isolates us.

And when it is shared,
it no longer belongs only to us.

May this be a space
where those wounds find a name,
rest, and meaning.

Because healing does not always mean
that the pain disappears.

Sometimes, healing begins
when we understand
that we are not alone—
and that a more just world is not something we wait for:

it is something we build, little by little, together.

"When society learns to see with respect,
the wounds carried by our families begin to heal."

✦

4.

Defending What We Love

"One mother who raises her voice can open a path; many mothers together can change the world."

The Voice of Mothers as a Force for Change

There comes a moment—sometimes clear, sometimes almost imperceptible—when something inside us changes.

After walking for so long through diagnoses, doubts, and silence, we stop trying merely to survive… and begin to raise our voices.

Many of the advances in inclusion that today seem ordinary did not begin in offices or public policy.

They were born in waiting rooms, at school meetings, in uncomfortable conversations where mothers and fathers decided that their love for their children was stronger than silence.

This is how a different kind of path begins.

We come from chapters where we faced, head-on, the unseen wounds, the judgment of others, the weight of uncertainty, and the exhaustion that is rarely spoken aloud.

And then, almost without realizing it, something profound happens:

we discover that the love we have for our children does not only sustain us… it also moves us forward.
None of us chose this path.

We never imagined ourselves explaining diagnoses, navigating systems, searching for services, facing visible barriers and others no one names.
We did not grow up thinking that one day we would become interpreters, advocates, and mediators between our children and a world that is still not prepared to see them as they deserve.

And yet, here we are.
And although we arrived with fear, with doubts, and with nights full of questions, love did what it always does:

it transformed.
It transformed us.

That love that sometimes feels fragile turns out to be one of the greatest forces that exist.

A force that pulled us out of silence when speaking hurt.
A force that taught us that love alone is not enough:
we must also open doors, knock on others, insist on some, and tear down the ones that should never have been closed.

In that process, we discovered something no one explained to us, but life taught us clearly:
as mothers, we are not only our children's first teachers—
we are the first to truly know them.

We are the first to read their gestures, understand their fears, celebrate their attempts.
The first specialists—not in law or medicine—
but in them:

in their unique way of learning,
in what they need to move forward,
in what they can achieve with the right support and constant love.

We know every step forward, every setback, every sign others overlook.
We know when something is not right and when something deserves to be celebrated.

And for that reason—precisely for that reason—
we cannot remain silent.

Our children need a voice that speaks when they still cannot.
A voice that asks, insists, accompanies, and defends their right to belong.

With time, we realize that we have become that voice.
A voice that asks questions when others remain silent.
That demands when others minimize.
That explains when necessary, but also knows how to say "enough" when respect is at risk.

A voice that learns to navigate schools, hospitals, offices, meetings, evaluations, and complex systems.
A voice that, even when it trembles, remains steady because it knows who it is speaking for.

Being the mother of a child with a disability does not make us experts in law or professional therapists.
But it transforms us into something just as powerful—perhaps even more so:

women who do not give up.

Women who learn, ask, search, document, advocate, insist… and insist again.
Who celebrate a returned phone call, an approved appointment, a teacher who listens, a space that finally says "yes."

We are not perfect or unbreakable.
We are still afraid, still tired, still full of doubts.
But now we know something we may not have known at the beginning:

silence leaves emptiness;
speaking—even when it is difficult—opens paths.

Paths for our children,
and for those who will come after them.

This chapter is a recognition of that strength born from love.

Of that courage that is not learned in courses or books,
but in real life,
day by day.

Of that voice that once trembled
and today is clearer, stronger, and truly ours.

Here begins the part of the journey where we will also listen to other mothers.
Women who have defended, fallen, and risen again.
Who have cried and celebrated.
Who have knocked on doors and, at times, brought down walls.

Their stories are not meant to move through drama,
but to accompany through truth.

Because defending what we love is, in the end, one of the most human acts that exists.

And in that act,
whether we intended to or not,
we discover a voice we never knew we had.

The Voice No One Expected

They say motherhood changes us,
but being the mother of a child with a disability transforms us in ways few people truly understand.

It is not a sudden or immediate change.
It is something that awakens slowly.

Sometimes from anger, sometimes from fear,
but always from love.
That fierce love we never imagined we could feel.

At first, we speak softly.
Carefully.
With doubt.
With that feeling of not knowing whether we have the right to question, to ask, to demand.

We wonder if we are overreacting.
If it is okay to make others uncomfortable.
If maybe it would be better to stay silent.

But all it takes is one moment:
an unfair comment,
a door that will not open,
a right someone tries to deny…

And then, without warning, something emerges that we never imagined we had: a voice.

A voice that is firm and clear,
that does not seek conflict or attention,

but justice and dignity.

A voice that was always there,
asleep beneath layers of insecurity,
waiting for the moment when the need became greater than the fear.

And in that moment,
something even deeper happens:
the lioness awakens.

That instinctive strength that needs no training and no permission.
That part of us that recognizes danger before anyone else,
that feels injustice in the skin
and rises to protect what it loves.

It does not roar to intimidate.
It does not attack for the sake of attacking.
It defends because it knows that lives, rights, and dignity are at stake.

Many of us did not know that lioness lived within us,
but she was always there,
waiting for the moment to emerge.

No one taught us how to use this voice.
We did not grow up thinking we would face educational, medical, or administrative systems.

Nor did we dream of becoming translators of diagnoses,
interpreters of reports,
or mediators between professionals who do not always listen.
And yet, one day, we find ourselves there:
speaking from a place we did not know,

with a firmness that surprises even those who once believed we were quiet or shy.

This voice appears in the most unexpected places:

— In a school meeting, when we explain why our children belong in the classroom just as much as any other child.
— In a hospital, when we ask for respect and care before speed.
— Within the family, when we make it clear that our children do not need pity, but real support.
— In the community, when we question practices that exclude without intention… but exclude all the same.

And the most surprising thing is that this voice, born from a personal struggle, does not only open paths for our children.
It also opens them for others.
Because when one mother stands with dignity,
others begin to feel they can do the same.

Disability rights advocates such as Judith Heumann have pointed out for decades that many advances in inclusion begin exactly this way: when someone dares to raise their voice against an injustice that once seemed normal.

When one mother names what no one else was saying, another discovers she is not alone.
When one says, "This is not right," another hears, "I have the right to ask for more too."

With time, we come to understand that this voice is not new.
It was always there.
In every act of protection,
in every instinct, in every sleepless night.

It only needed a reason to be heard.
And our children—
their lives, their rights, their dignity—
became that reason.

We are not experts in law or professional therapists.
We are not trained teachers.
But we are the ones who know our children better than anyone else.

We are the ones who know when something is not right,
when something is being denied,
when something needs to change.

We are their voice when the world does not want to listen.
That is why this voice surprises others…
but not us.

Because we know where it was born:
from the only place where real struggles are born.
From love.
Love that defends.
Love that opens paths.
Love that refuses to stay silent.

The voice no one expected is, in truth,
the voice that had always been waiting for us to dare to use it.

And now that we have found it—
and awakened the lioness within us—we are not going to let it go.

Because a voice born from love will always find a way to be heard.

Learning to Advocate Without a Degree

There comes a moment on this journey when something shifts.
A moment when you realize that loving your child also means learning to defend them.

None of us ever imagined taking on this role.

We never thought that one day we would need to learn about laws, protocols, school policies, educational rights, medical requirements, or processes that seem written in another language.

We did not grow up thinking we would learn how to interpret reports, challenge evaluations, or question decisions made about our children's lives.

But a diagnosis changed the course of everything,
and what once felt distant suddenly became urgent.

Almost overnight, what we never learned in a classroom, we learned in real life—
with necessity as our teacher and love as our fuel.

One day we are receiving the news, trying to understand terms we had never heard before…
and the next, we are filling out forms, reading evaluations, taking notes during meetings where everything sounds complex, formal, distant.

We learn to gather paperwork no one explained to us.
To ask for copies no one offered.
To make phone calls that seem never-ending.
We learn to translate medical, legal, and administrative language

to understand what each word truly means in our children's everyday lives.

And here, one of the deepest wounds of this journey appears:
having to describe our children through their difficulties.

We learn—with pain—to listen as deficits are listed:
limitations, delays, risks.

To hear entire lives reduced to what they "cannot do,"
what they "have not achieved,"
what is "missing."

And even though we know this is often necessary to access support and services,
it still hurts.
Because no mother wants her child to be presented as a problem that needs to be justified.

This constant exercise leaves a mark.
It feels like a quiet betrayal committed in the name of love.

Because we know that without those reports, without those harsh words,
the system does not open its doors.

We become persistent.
Not because we want to be difficult,
but because we understand that if we do not ask, no one will ask for us.

We become brave.
Not because fear disappears,

but because fear becomes smaller when we know who we are fighting for.

And we become stubborn…
in that beautiful kind of stubbornness that is born when we understand that behind every form, every appointment, every signature,
there is a real opportunity for our children.

Every process becomes a small but meaningful battle.

A rescheduled appointment.
A service denied without explanation.
An incomplete evaluation.

A recommendation that does not reflect what we see and live every single day.
A school asking for patience,
when all we are asking for is justice.

And yes, it hurts.

It hurts to realize that basic rights—healthcare, education, support, accessibility—do not come automatically.
It hurts to feel that the burden falls on our shoulders.
That we must prove, again and again,
that our children deserve what every child deserves.

It hurts to discover that this path requires constant vigilance,
attention to every detail,
because one oversight, one omission, or one "we'll see later"
can cost valuable opportunities.
This is not a heroic role.
It is not a medal.

It is not a romantic mission.

It is real exhaustion.
Accumulated wear and tear.
Learning to navigate difficult conversations
while continuing to be mothers, partners, workers, human beings.

And still… we keep going.

Because we know that every document submitted,
every email sent, every uncomfortable meeting,
every word defended
is a step toward a more dignified future for our children.

Because we understand that no one will fight with the same devotion as a mother.

Because we are their legal representatives, yes…
but also their emotional ones.

We are their voice in spaces where they cannot yet speak.
Their momentum when the system stalls.
Their defense when the world does not understand.

And along the way, we discover something essential: we are not alone.

There are other mothers carrying folders full of paperwork,
notebooks filled with notes,
calendars covered with appointments and unanswered calls,
the same exhaustion in their eyes…
and the same determination in their hearts.

We meet in waiting rooms,
in school meetings, in hallways,
in support groups, on social media,
in any space where this kind of motherhood brings us together
without needing introductions.

Together, we learn, share, warn, and celebrate.

Each mother who raises her voice leaves a door slightly open for the next.
Each mother who insists widens the path so others do not stumble as much.

And all of us, through our everyday struggles,
are building something we may never fully see,
but that we know will matter for those who come after us.

Being "advocates without a title" is not a role we chose.
But it is a profound act of love.
A quiet, exhausting, brave, and necessary act.

Because our children deserve justice.
They deserve access.
They deserve real opportunities.

And while the world learns to offer those things on its own,
we will remain here:
with steady voices, open hearts,
and the unwavering conviction that all this effort—
even if no one applauds it—
is worth it.

Every Milestone, a Battle Won

For many families, an achievement is something visible:
a ceremony, a medal, public recognition,
a moment shared in photos
and celebrated without explanation.

For us, mothers of children with disabilities,
achievements are different.

They are intimate.
Quiet.
Sometimes almost imperceptible from the outside…
but within our hearts,
they feel as vast as the universe.

A milestone might be that step that comes after months of exercises
that seem endless.
Or a word spoken with such effort
that it feels as though you spoke it alongside them.

It might be a gaze that finally lingers.
A moment of connection so brief
that only we understand everything it holds.

It might be that small act of independence
that no one else noticed…
but that you saw like a star beginning to shine.

Each of those milestones carries a story.

A story of hands guiding with patience.

Of therapists who walk beside us.
Of sleepless nights.
Of repeated explanations.
Of days when it felt like nothing was moving forward
and then, suddenly,
a small miracle breaks through the routine.

To the world, it may not seem extraordinary.
To us, it confirms something deep and undeniable: it is worth it.
The accumulated exhaustion is worth it.
The hours spent in waiting rooms.
The endless paperwork.
The therapies. The tears that were not always seen.

None of it falls on barren ground when that moment arrives—
the moment when something finally begins to bloom.

Our children do not follow the world's timeline.
Their path does not always match
what others expect or consider "normal."

And still—or perhaps because of that—
every step they take carries immense strength
and an effort that deserves to be honored.

That is why every milestone matters so deeply:
because it comes wrapped in perseverance,
repetition, patience,
sustained hope, and a love that refuses to give up.

It is true that society often cannot fully grasp what lies behind these victories.
Sometimes, we even keep them to ourselves.
Not because they are unimportant,

but because we do not always know where to place them.

While other mothers speak about awards, grades, diplomas, or performances,
our victories live in the everyday—
in details that do not always fit into ordinary conversation.

A victory might be staying in a place a little longer without distress.
Accepting a new texture without anxiety.
Allowing a haircut without fear.
Sleeping through the night.
No longer needing a medication or a medical device.

These are victories that are not applauded publicly,
but to us, they mean the world.

And if we often hold them quietly within us,
it is not because we are any less proud,
but because we sense that few people would truly understand
everything that made them possible.
But we know.
We know the accumulated effort.
The pain carried in silence.
The faith that sustains us when progress comes slowly.
The courage that keeps us moving even on difficult days.
Everything that is given
so that one small step can exist.

That is why, for us,
every milestone is much more than progress.

It is a battle won.
A flag that quietly waves within us,

reminding us that yes, it is possible,
that yes, it is worth it,
that our children hold an immense potential
that cannot be measured by statistics or predictions.

And so, we continue.

With hearts full of small victories
the world does not always see,
but that sustain us
and help us keep moving forward.

Step by step.
Without giving up.

Because every milestone—no matter how small it may seem—
carries within it the strength of love
that sustains us
and keeps us connected.

From Wound to Collective Voice

The diagnosis often arrives like a sudden blow—
a rupture that leaves us looking around, unsure of where to turn.

In those first days, the world seems to shrink:
it feels as though no one understands, no one has lived through the same thing, and our pain is ours alone.
Life seems to have pushed us into a place with no map and no companions.

But time—and experience—slowly reveal something we cannot see at first:
we are not alone. Our story is not the only one.

What once felt like a desert of loneliness
slowly begins to fill with quiet presences:
mothers who are also learning, fighting, falling, and getting back up again.

There are women, in different places and facing different diagnoses,
fighting battles that feel deeply familiar.
Some advocate for inclusion in classrooms where doors still close without meaning to.
Others keep insisting until a specialist truly listens.
Others fight for their children's right to services, support, and care that should never have been denied.

And in each of them, there is something we recognize—
as though we are looking into an unexpected mirror.

Their challenges may not be exactly the same as ours,

but they share the same root:
love that turns into action,
exhaustion that does not stop us,
fear that does not paralyze us,
and the deep conviction that our children deserve far more
than the world is often prepared to offer them.

Without planning it, without even searching for it,
we begin to recognize one another.
We begin speaking a language that can only be learned by living this life.

And that is where something begins to grow—
something no theory can fully explain,
but the soul can feel: sisterhood.

The kind of empathy that exists only among those who carry similar wounds.
The relief of finding another mother who also learned to fill out forms without instructions,
who also placed dreams on hold in order to become an expert out of necessity,
who also carried guilt for things that were never hers to carry.

Suddenly, hearing another mother say "me too"
has the power to mend deep cracks within us.

And little by little, from that first loneliness,
a community begins to take shape.
A network that is never formally announced, yet undeniably real.
A collective strength capable of supporting, guiding, inspiring, and opening paths.

Because when one mother dares to speak, another finds courage.

When one shares her experience, another realizes she is not wrong. When one achieves progress for her child, she creates space for others to follow.

That is when we begin to understand
that our struggles do not remain within the walls of our homes.

That school meeting where we defended a right,
that request we submitted a thousand times,
that uncomfortable conversation we carried with dignity,
that door we kept pushing until it finally opened…
none of it benefits only our children—
it also benefits the children of other mothers.

From individual pain, a collective voice is born.

A voice that says:
enough of limiting perspectives,
enough of systems that exclude,
enough of believing that a diagnosis defines a destiny.

A voice that reminds the world of something essential:
our children are not walking diagnoses,
not clinical cases,
not stories meant to be pitied.

They are whole human beings—
with value, with rights, and with a rightful place in this world.
And we, far from being victims or "special" mothers in an empty sense,
are women who have learned to transform every doubt into learning,
every tear into momentum,

and every obstacle into a reason to keep going.
When our voices come together,
inclusion stops being just an ideal—
and begins to take shape.

Because mothers know something society is still learning:
no struggle is small when dignity is at stake,
and no mother walks alone
when another chooses to walk beside her.

Sometimes we do not move forward quickly.
Sometimes we move forward exhausted.

But we move forward together.
And when we do,
the path—though still difficult—
no longer feels quite so dark.

Before We Continue…

At the beginning of this journey, many of us believed we had no voice.

We were ordinary mothers with ordinary concerns, living lives that felt steady… until a diagnosis shook the ground beneath our feet.

In that moment, shyness blurred into fear, silence turned into uncertainty, and loneliness wrapped itself around us without warning.

But with time—and often through tears and exhaustion—we discovered something none of us had imagined: within us, there was a dormant strength, a voice that was never seeking applause or approval, but justice, dignity, and real opportunities for our children.

That voice led us to learn things we never imagined we would need to know.
We did not study law, yet we learned to navigate regulations.
We were not trained in special education, yet we came to understand reports, evaluations, and goals.
We are not doctors, yet we learned to navigate diagnoses, therapies, treatments, and adaptations.

Almost overnight, we became specialists in what matters most: our children, their rights, and their needs.
What strengthens them.
What challenges them.
What they need in order to keep growing.
And above all, we became their voice.
The voice that opens doors when others close them.

The voice that explains when the world does not understand.
The voice that stands firm when others question their worth.

And in the middle of so much daily struggle…
small signs began to appear—the kind that sustain the soul.
Not grand celebrations or public recognition, but those intimate moments that only a mother can recognize as quiet miracles:

an attempt that once seemed impossible,
a new gesture after weeks of effort,
a small step forward that no one else would notice unless they were looking with the heart,
a calmer day,
a look of accomplishment on our children's faces that brings back our breath—and our hope.

Each of those moments reminded us of something essential:
that our children move forward in their own way,
that effort does leave a mark,
that consistency creates paths where none existed before,
and that love can carry us through every battle—even on the hardest days.

But it is also important to say this clearly and with care:
Defending what we love does not mean we all walk the same path.
Even when diagnoses are similar, no story is ever the same.

Some mothers learn to carry not only their children,
but wheelchairs, oxygen tanks, breathing equipment, or feeding systems that must go everywhere with them.
Others search, again and again, for dignified spaces to change a child who no longer fits on a table designed only for babies.

Some live in constant alert because their children may run without

warning, put themselves in danger within seconds, or become lost easily.
Others carefully manage every gesture, every stimulus, every environment, trying to prevent crises that may end in aggression, self-harm, or the misunderstanding gaze of others.

Our realities are as diverse as our children's bodies, minds, and stories.
And still, there is something that deeply unites us:
the need to feel accompanied, understood, and validated.

Not compared.
Not measured.
Not judged by the visible—or invisible—weight of what we carry.

Because motherhood is not defined by the equipment we transport or by the behaviors others observe from the outside.
It is defined by the love that sustains it.
And so, what began as an individual struggle slowly became something collective.

We discovered we were not alone.
That there were other mothers, in other places, crossing the same storms, asking the same questions, holding onto the same hopes, defending the same truths.
And that is where something beautiful happened:

the wound became a voice,
and the voice became a community.

A community that does not give up.
That does not accept injustice as normal.
That understands that love does not remain still—it moves,

transforms, and opens the way.
Defending what we love wove us together.

It made us stronger.
It made us a bridge for the mothers who will come after us.
It made us hope for a world that still needs to learn about dignity, inclusion, and respect.

And so, from our very different stories, a shared truth was born:
we do not need to compete over who suffers more.

We need to walk beside one another, because no one should have to carry this alone.

Pain is not measured by diagnoses,
by what is visible,
or by what others consider "more severe."

Every form of motherhood carries its own battles.

Some are visible at first glance.
Others remain hidden behind bodies that appear "typical" and lives no one imagines to be complex.
Comparison isolates us.
Connection restores our humanity.

And when we stop measuring who struggles more and begin walking together, the weight is shared, guilt becomes lighter, and the wound no longer hurts in solitude.

"From a single voice born in pain,
a chorus of love rises—one that will never fall silent."

✦

5.

Voices That Walk With Us

"A mother's story is not meant to be compared—
it is meant to intertwine with others,
reminding us that no one walks alone."

Stories of Love, Struggle, and Shared Hope

This book was born from a simple yet profound purpose:
to accompany.

To accompany the mother who, upon hearing a diagnosis,
felt the ground open beneath her feet.
The mother who saves her tears for the quiet of the night
because during the day, there is no space to fall apart.

The mother who feels lost among reports, therapies, appointments,
and prognoses that seem written in another language.
The mother who keeps moving forward,
even while trembling inside.

But this book was never meant to remain only in my voice.

Because no single story is enough
when we speak of this kind of motherhood.
Because there are many of us.
Because our struggles, though different,
recognize one another like reflections.
Because our wounds resemble one another…
and so does our strength.

That is why this chapter is a gift.

A gift offered by real women
who, at some point, chose to open their hearts
and share what they have lived alongside their children.
There is no theory here. No speeches.
There is life.
Life that hurts, teaches, and transforms.

Life written between therapies, fears, stacks of paperwork, sleepless nights, and the quiet miracles of everyday life.
Each mother in these pages carries within her an entire universe:
her light, her shadows, her breaking points, and her rebirths.

Some faced devastating diagnoses.
Others walked in darkness, not knowing what was happening.
Others fought against systems that were never prepared to receive their children.
And all of them—without exception—
learned to love beyond exhaustion
and to rise again even when no strength seemed left.

Some of the stories you are about to read also come through the voices of fathers,
who, in their own ways, have also walked, cared for, and carried this journey alongside their families.
Their words are part of this shared experience,
because disability does not live in one person alone—
it moves through entire families, transforms relationships,
and reshapes love in all its forms.

And it is precisely within that love—lived, sustained, and shared—
that we discover something that deeply connects us all:
that loneliness becomes lighter when a story is shared,
that shame begins to dissolve when someone says, "me too,"
and that exhaustion is honored when another mother understands it without explanation.
There is something profoundly human
about the moment someone dares to tell their story
and discovers that another heart understands.

Educator Parker Palmer once wrote that the human soul does not

need to be "fixed," but simply to be seen and heard.
And that is exactly what happens when one story finds another.

These are voices that accompany.
Voices that hold. Voices that validate.
Voices that bring light into spaces where silence once lived.
Voices that, when joined together, become a living, resilient network
where no one is left behind.

Today, I invite you to read them with an open heart.
Not only to know their stories,
but to feel the embrace within each one.
Because behind every testimony
there is a powerful reminder:
we are not alone, we never were,
and we never will be again.

Go on.

May these voices find you,
walk with you,
and hold you—
just as they did for me.

The testimonies you are about to read
have been generously shared by the families
who agreed to be part of these pages.

Some names and identifying details have been changed
to protect their privacy,
but each story preserves, intact,
the truth of what was lived
and the love that continues to sustain it.

Before Fear, There Was Love

There are stories that do not begin with fear, but with hope. Imelda's story begins that way.

At 41, her second pregnancy arrived like a luminous surprise. It was not a pregnancy lived in anxiety, but in awareness and love. There were checkups, tests, and medical follow-ups. And there was also a conversation that would shape everything that followed.

Her gynecologist suggested she undergo an amniocentesis. Because of her age, he explained, there was a possibility that the baby could be born with a genetic condition—particularly Down syndrome—as well as other possible malformations.

Imelda listened carefully and responded with a simple but decisive question:

—If a condition is confirmed, can you reverse it or cure it?
—No, the doctor replied.

His explanation was clear: the purpose of the test was not to change anything, but to give her the option of deciding whether or not to continue the pregnancy.

Imelda did not hesitate. Her answer was calm and firm:

—I am not going to have an abortion. And I am not going to undergo that procedure.

Not because she denied the possibility,
but because her decision had already been made.

The pregnancy unfolded peacefully. Imelda prepared everything to welcome her baby with deep emotion: a beautiful bassinet for those first months, small details chosen with love, dreams and plans for the life that was on its way.

She was waiting with hope, not conditions.

And then the day arrived. It was a girl.
Paula was born.
Imelda remembers her exactly as she was from that very first moment: beautiful exactly as she was.

Imelda cried—not because of her daughter's condition,
but because of the possibility of not being enough…
of not having the knowledge needed to care for her, support her, and protect her the way she deserved.

That was when she spoke with God.
Not to complain. Not to ask why.

In that deep conversation, Imelda accepted her reality and asked for something different: that if she had been entrusted with the responsibility of being the mother of such a special child, she would also be given the guidance needed to offer Paula everything she would need.

The first months passed with relative calm, though not without challenges. Paula was born with a heart condition that resolved favorably around the age of two, without the need for major intervention.

Before that, there were hospital visits and moments of deep anguish, when Paula would stop breathing and fear would take over.

In both the good moments and the difficult ones,
her conversation with God never broke.

What did break, again and again,
was her trust in certain "professionals" who were supposed to guide and support her.

During one hospital visit, after confirming that Paula was stable, a doctor said—without the slightest empathy:

—"Don't worry, that's just how these mongoloids are," he said, using an outdated and deeply offensive term.

Imelda's anger and frustration were immediate.

And painfully, it would not be the last time.

Throughout Paula's life, some of the deepest moments of misunderstanding did not come from society at large,
but from those who, by training, were supposed to be allies on the path toward inclusion.

Another moment remained deeply marked in her memory.

When her maternity leave ended, Imelda planned to return to work and enroll Paula in a daycare where she had applied since pregnancy. Everything was ready.

The day she arrived holding her baby in her arms to finalize the process, the doctor looked at her and asked:

—Does she have Down syndrome?

Imelda responded, as she always did, with clarity:
—Are you asking me, or informing me?

The answer came immediately:

—I'm very sorry, but we cannot accept her. We do not have the resources to care for a child like that.

Similar experiences followed later, as Paula entered the school system.

The pattern repeated itself again and again: seeing the label before the person. Deciding in advance. Never taking the time to see the abilities, the talents, and the humanity standing right in front of them.

Alongside all of this came a deep loneliness.
Paula's father decided—without ever saying it directly—that he was not ready for an experience like this.
He did not stay.

And although Imelda continued forward with strength, she acknowledges that walking this path without her daughter's father has been one of the hardest parts.

A reality repeated in many stories of disability and motherhood: not all fathers are able to hold the weight of the challenge—or recognize the gift—this kind of parenthood can be.

Today, Paula is a joyful, intelligent young girl, full of life.

She loves sharing joyful moments with her mother; they are inseparable companions. She deeply enjoys music—especially singing—and has a natural talent for design and drawing.

It is no coincidence: her mother is both a painter and an architect. It runs in her blood.

One of Imelda's dreams is to find a place where Paula can take real fashion design classes—not symbolic activities, but true training—because she enjoys it and clearly shows the ability.

When Imelda looks back on her journey, she describes it as a path sustained by constant dialogue with God, by love, companionship, and a deep sense of gratitude.

Over time, she has come to see Paula as her good-luck charm. With her by her side, she says, things flow, align, and fall into place with a kind of ease she cannot fully explain—but deeply recognizes and honors.

In her conversations with God, Imelda has never asked Him to change His plans.
She has only shared one quiet, intimate desire—spoken softly, with an open heart:
that if possible, they would never have to be apart.

She does not want to leave Paula alone,
nor can she imagine existing without her.

Imelda describes herself as "ignorant"—not from lack, but from humility. She acknowledges she does not know everything, but she affirms something with conviction: she has always been willing to learn, especially everything related to Down syndrome.

For her, learning has been another way of loving.
At the end of her testimony, Imelda speaks to other mothers of children with disabilities.

Not from theory, nor from idealization,
but from lived experience.

She says that, as human beings, we spend our lives searching for love: we want to love, to be loved, and to receive love from others. She herself once asked God to help her understand what true love is.

And she found it.

She found it when she became Paula's mother.

For Imelda, her daughter embodies true love:
a love without conditions, without demands, without expectations to fulfill.

A love that asks for nothing in return,
and yet gives everything.

That is why her message to other mothers is not to search for something outside themselves, but to learn to recognize, accept, and live that love when it appears in forms that do not always resemble what we once imagined.

Through her daughter, Imelda did not only learn how to love.
She learned how to receive true love.

The Procedure that Changed Everything

Although every diagnosis is different, the emotions we experience as mothers are universal.

Here, Aracely opens her heart to share how she has lived Osvaldo's journey, with the hope that her voice may accompany other women who are feeling the same today.

This is her story:

There are memories that never fade.
Aracely can return to that day exactly.
Osvaldo was about to turn one year old.

He was a healthy baby.
He could already stand on his own.
He was beginning to take his first steps.
He was in that beautiful stage where everything feels like discovery.

They would drive around in the truck, and he would blow at the traffic lights, convinced he could change them with his breath.
She would hold him in his seat, laughing as she let him believe he could move the world with his breath.

There were no signs.
No suspicions.
No pending diagnoses.
Everything was fine.

She took him to a routine physical check-up.
The doctor examined everything.

—"He's perfectly fine."

That was the phrase.

He only added one more thing: he recommended a circumcision. Something simple. Quick. Scheduled.

"Come in at eight, and he'll be home by eleven."

Nothing extraordinary.
They trusted.
The procedure was done in Mexico.
He was given general anesthesia.
The surgery ended.

And Osvaldo did not wake up.
Instead of crying, instead of opening his eyes, he began to seize.

—"He wasn't even crying… he just lay there, unresponsive," Aracely recalls.

At first, they were told he was simply taking a little longer to come out of the anesthesia. Later, they suggested he might have suffered a previous injury that could have contributed to what was happening.
But there had been no injury.
The seizures would not stop.

When he was finally transferred to El Paso and underwent more extensive testing, what no one was prepared to hear was confirmed: during the procedure, there had been a respiratory failure.
At some point, he stopped receiving oxygen.
His brain suffered hypoxia.

The damage would be irreversible.

The hypoxia affected his motor system. He was left with paralysis on the right side of his body, which is why he does everything with his left hand.

His right eye was affected.
His speech.
His vocal cords.
The seizures began that same day, and ever since, they have remained part of his life and require ongoing treatment.

And the little boy who was just beginning to walk… stopped.

That is a different kind of grief.

It is not about what never was.
It is about what was already beginning… and suddenly stopped.
It was not a prenatal diagnosis.
It was not a congenital condition.
It was not an illness that gradually progressed.

It was something unexpected. Devastating.
A "simple" procedure that shattered the story of a young family and their first child.
When they explained that the damage was irreversible, Aracely felt as though her world had collapsed.

And she blamed herself.
For years.
One thought haunted her constantly:
"If I hadn't taken him…"
She was seventeen years old.
Her husband worked.
Reality arrived all at once.

After the hospitalization came more tests, neurologists, unimaginable medical expenses, and constant uncertainty.
But alongside the guilt, something stronger appeared: the instinct to fight.

By the time Osvaldo was a year and a half old, the search had already begun.

Therapies.
Schools.
Resources.
Information.

She became involved as a volunteer.
She learned medical terminology.
She learned how to explain hypoxia.
She learned how to advocate for her son.
Her fear was not only medical.

Her greatest fear was not knowing what Osvaldo would be able to do in life.
Not finding something in which he could truly thrive.
Not having enough strength to support him academically, emotionally, and socially.
And there was another fear she speaks about with complete honesty:

She thought she did not want to have more children.

A fixed thought settled into her mind:
How could she care for other children if Osvaldo needed all of her time?
What if she was not enough for everyone?
That fear was real. Deep.

It was not a lack of love.
It was the awareness of the level of dedication her son required.

With time, and as life continued moving forward…
Five years later, her second child was born.
And instead of becoming another burden, he became a gift.

From the very beginning, he became one of Osvaldo's greatest companions.
Her third child was born when Osvaldo was twelve.
Aracely always taught her children respect and pride.

They have never diminished him.
They love him exactly as he is.

At home, they do not talk about "what he lacks," but about what he *can* do.
And he can do a great deal.

Osvaldo learned to read.
He fought very hard for it.

Over time, he lost that ability. They are not sure whether it was due to visual impairment or neurological changes. He continues in treatment.

He takes medication to control the seizures.
He is highly susceptible to infections; even a simple cold can trigger a crisis.

He has also struggled with hip problems.
At twenty-three, he needed an implant.

Insurance initially refused to approve it because, according to them, "those surgeries were for older people."
Another administrative battle added to the medical ones.
Eventually, Aracely succeeded.
The surgery was approved, and Osvaldo received his implant.

Those were incredibly difficult days.
At that same time, Aracely herself was going through cervical surgery.

There were days of profound exhaustion.
Days when she asked God why.

There were difficult years at school as well.
Behavioral crises.
Moments of frustration because he could not express himself.
Mood changes during adolescence.
Times when he became angry with her.

Because with a mother, that is where everything is released.
Because she is the one who sets boundaries.

—"Even if others see him as calm, a mother is the one who has to say what is right or wrong, and she always ends up being the bad one," she says honestly.

With the right medication, many things stabilized.

And little by little, moments of light began to return.
In high school, he participated in the Special Olympics.

He swam across Olympic-size pools.
He went to the World Games.
He won medals.

He played soccer.
He appeared in the newspaper.

Aracely watched him swim and understood that the story had not ended on the day of the hypoxia.

Osvaldo has an incredible ability to build Lego sets with thousands of tiny pieces. He loves them.
He completes enormous puzzles in record time—and genuinely enjoys doing it.
He concentrates deeply.

He enjoys life.
He is patient.
He is focused.
He is happy.
And that matters deeply to her.
She repeats it often:

"He is happy."

Today, her greatest fear is no longer the hypoxia.
It is not the seizures.
It is the future.

Preparing him for the day when she is no longer here.

Hoping he may one day become independent… while also fearing that the world may not fully understand him.

It is a constant inner struggle.

Her husband has lived the experience from a different place—more focused on work, repeating that everything would eventually be okay.

Each of them has carried this journey as best they could.

When Aracely looks back, she recognizes the tragedy.

She does not minimize it.
She does not romanticize it.
It was devastating.

But she also recognizes the good people who appeared along the way.

Her mother-in-law, who helped from the very beginning.
The family members who supported them.
The resources they eventually found.

And she leaves a message for other mothers.

Her message comes from lived experience—and from the heart:

Do not remain paralyzed by pain.
Do not lose time only suffering.
Seek resources. Time matters.
Accept the pain, but keep moving forward.

And above all:
You are not alone.

Because for her, beyond the medical damage, the hardest part was the loneliness.

The judgment in the street.
At the bank.
At school.

Comments from people who do not understand that behind a behavior, there is a brain injury.

She wishes someone had told her, in those early days:
You are not alone.

Today, she says it for others.

And when she speaks about her son, she does not speak from tragedy.

She speaks from this truth:

"I can't say he's lucky to have me… but I can say I'm lucky to have him."

Because Osvaldo is not only the little boy who stopped breathing that day.

He is the young man who learned to live in a different way.

He is the son who taught her that happiness does not always move in a straight line.

He is proof that a life can change in a single moment…
and still hold meaning.

Looking at Our Son, Not the Diagnosis

This testimony is born from two voices walking side by side.

It is the story a father and a mother share from different places, but with the same intention: to tell what it has meant to accompany their son's life through love, uncertainty, and daily perseverance.

When Junior was born, they were both very young parents. Like many at that stage of life, they were learning how to be parents while life moved quickly around them. They had no experience, no clear references, no apparent reason to think something might be wrong.

Their son was growing, playing, simply being a child at home.
In those early years, nothing seemed out of the ordinary.

It was with time—and as they themselves grew, matured, and learned—that they began to understand that being parents was not only about caring, but also about observing, listening, and learning to read what is not always spoken with words.

They began to notice that Junior was not developing at the same pace as other children.
He was not speaking.

When he entered kindergarten, his teachers also noticed differences: the lack of communication, difficulties with socialization, and the fact that he was not progressing at the same level as other children his age.

That realization awakened fear and uncertainty.
His father admits that his greatest fear was not the diagnosis itself, but not knowing what to do or where to seek help for his son.

They knew very little about diagnoses, therapies, or alternative paths forward. They had no map and no clear answers.
They only knew that something was not unfolding the way they had expected… and that they had no idea where to begin.

His mother, meanwhile, says she already sensed something was not right, even if she could not yet explain exactly what it was.
The first diagnosis mentioned only attention deficit disorder.
It reflected what was most visible at the time, but it did not fully explain what they were living through.

That was when an intense period of searching began:
searching for information, consultations, and answers that might help them understand the signs that were only beginning to take shape.
And alongside that search came a kind of pain that is not always spoken aloud:
misunderstanding.

Not only from society—which often looks without truly understanding—but also from the people closest to them.

The kind of misunderstanding that hurts the most:
the misunderstanding within one's own family.
Explaining the same things over and over again.
Justifying what should never have needed justification.

Feeling that even the people who were supposed to support them could not fully understand what they were living.
Both parents agree that this became one of the hardest parts of the journey.

His mother says it plainly:

the misunderstanding and rejection they experienced within their own family left them feeling frustrated, hurt, and deeply alone.

Over time, daily life began to change.

They learned how to accompany their son, how to communicate with him, how to observe him more carefully and with fewer outside expectations.

His father explains that little by little, he learned how to relate better to his son—and at the same time, how to stop carrying the weight of society's judgment and the opinions of others.
The final diagnosis came years later.

By then, many things were already in motion.
They had already learned how to support him, adapt alongside him, and grow with him.
The name of the condition—which confirmed that Junior was also on the autism spectrum—did not change the love or effort they had already been building as parents.

The journey had not begun with a diagnosis.
It had begun long before that:
in everyday life.
In love.

There were milestones that became everyday miracles.
Junior developed language.

He always showed a remarkable willingness to face the challenges connected to his condition.
He grew up, graduated from high school, and earned his driver's license.

Today, he has a job where he is valued and appreciated.
Each of those accomplishments was the result of constant effort, close support, and a perseverance that never gave up.

But not everything has been easy.

What exhausts them the most, they admit, is society's lack of understanding toward people with disabilities.
And what worries them most is still the future:

Who will be with him?
Who will support him?
Who will care for him when they no longer can?

It is a question that remains open, without clear answers, and one they have learned to live with.

And still, when they speak about their son, they do so with love and pride.

Today, Junior is a young man with immense tenderness.
He is a loyal friend, a responsible employee,
someone people can trust.

He loves building Lego sets and has a collection of special sneakers that he cares for enthusiastically.

He enjoys the things he loves in his own way,
with a faithfulness to himself that few people manage to preserve.

Both parents agree on something essential:
Their son has taught them far more than they ever imagined possible.

He taught them not to give up, to value every step forward, and to look beyond other people's expectations.
His father summarizes it in words that run through this entire story:

"My son has taught me what no book ever could: never give up on life, despite adversity."

At the end, when his mother is asked what she would say to other mothers who are just beginning this journey, she does not offer long speeches or complicated advice.

She offers one simple and honest word:
Patience.

That lesson does not appear in manuals or diagnoses.

It is built day by day:
through living together,
through waiting,
through a love that stays.
This testimony is not about perfection or easy roads.

It is about presence.

About continuing to accompany a child even when the world does not fully understand.

About looking at a child not through the lens of what is "missing," but through the fullness of the life that is already there.

And when that perspective changes,
it is not only their path that transforms.

Something within us transforms too.

A Promise Before She Ever Got to Hold Him

Rosario remembers that moment with a clarity time has never erased.
As if everything had stopped there.

She was lying on the operating table, staring at the aluminum surgical lights suspended above her. Reflected on their metallic surface, she could make out the doctors' movements as they worked during the C-section.

She was about to become a mother…
and she was alone.
Her husband had not made it in time. The long lines at the bridge between Ciudad Juárez and El Paso had kept him on the other side.
No one held her hand.
No one explained what was happening.

Rosario felt anxious. Sad too.
Not because of the baby—she had been waiting for him with excitement—
but because of the loneliness of that moment.

Even so, all her attention remained fixed on the instant her son would finally be born.
And then, it happened.
She saw him.
But she did not hear him cry.

That silence was the first thing that shook her soul.
The atmosphere shifted.
The voices became tense.
The expressions on the medical staff's faces changed.

Through her limited understanding of English, Rosario caught two words that landed in her chest like a blunt blow:
"Down syndrome."
She froze. In shock.

She pretended not to understand.
As if ignoring those words could somehow erase them.
Sadness flooded her before she could even process what was happening.
They did not place her son on her chest.
They did not bring him close for her to see him.
There was no first contact—the one she had imagined so many times.

They took him away without explanations, without comfort, without even a moment to say goodbye.
Only one thought crossed her mind:
This is a nightmare.

Her vital signs began to destabilize. Rosario started feeling unwell, and the medical staff placed an oxygen mask on her, trying to stabilize her while the procedure continued.
Her body reacted before her mind could understand.

No one stopped to explain what was happening, what those words meant, or what was happening with her son.
But deep inside, Rosario already knew:
This was not a bad dream.

When she was finally taken to her room, her husband was already there. On his face, she saw fear, confusion, and worry.
And in that moment, everything else lost importance.

She no longer wanted diagnoses.

She no longer wanted confirmations.
She only wanted to know whether her son was alive.
Whether he was safe.

Two days later, Rosario was finally allowed into the neonatal unit.
There was Christian.
So small. So fragile.
So different from what she had imagined, and at the same time, so completely hers.

She could not hold him.
She could not pull him close.
She could not protect him with her body the way she had longed to.
So she did the only thing she could:
She took his tiny hand and spoke to him.

She asked for forgiveness.
Forgiveness for wondering whether she had failed him somehow.
Forgiveness for fearing that her own body had not known how to protect him better.

Forgiveness—even though she knew, rationally, that this was a genetic condition.
It was a forgiveness born from love.
From the guilt so many mothers carry without reason.
From the instinctive desire to prevent any pain from touching their child.

The blow came again, even harder, when she was told that her son had a serious heart condition.
Added to that were his low weight and his difficulty breathing.
Christian would need surgery…
but only after gaining enough weight.

That was when, Rosario remembers clearly, something shifted inside her.
She stopped asking why
and began deciding how.

She asked God for forgiveness for having first worried about Down syndrome.
She asked forgiveness for her fear.
And she made a simple and absolute promise:

If her son was allowed to survive,
he would never go without love, care, or presence.

She did not ask for him to be "normal."
She did not ask for him to be extraordinary.
She only asked for him to be healthy and happy.

After the open-heart surgery, life took a decisive turn.
Christian healed.
The emergency visits stopped.
His breathing stabilized.
His heart recovered.

And then another stage began:
discovering who Christian was beyond fear, beyond the diagnosis, beyond the expectations others had placed on him.

Christian remained hospitalized for fifteen days.
Rosario barely left that chair.
It was not until he was stable—just before being discharged—that her own body finally collapsed.
High blood pressure. Swollen legs.

God, she says, held her together while she cared for her son.

And only when he no longer needed constant care, she became the one who needed to be cared for.

Rosario and her family made a conscious decision:
to raise Christian like their other children, understanding he might learn more slowly, but fully believing he would learn.

Because many times, she recalls, it is some doctors and specialists who speak in absolutes, describing futures filled only with "he won't be able to."

That was not Christian's story.

The milestones began to arrive one by one, like little lights appearing along the way.
Recovering remarkably fast from open-heart surgery at only four months old.
Learning to use the bathroom.
Proving he could hear, even when some tests claimed otherwise.
Saying "I love you."
Holding a pencil for the first time.

And there is one moment Rosario still holds as sacred within her motherhood.
When Christian was two weeks old, she was finally allowed to take him out of the incubator.
She had been told she would not be able to breastfeed him because his palate was too high and he would not be able to latch.

Rosario placed him gently against her chest, spoke softly to him, encouraged him.
Despite being so tiny and having so little strength, he latched on.
It lasted only a few minutes.

But it remained engraved in her memory forever.

Then came the part of the journey no one fully explains.
The part where a mother learns to see differently.
Where other people's looks begin to weigh heavily.
Where comments—sometimes disguised as curiosity, sometimes as mockery—hurt more than they should.

Rosario remembers asking God for tolerance.
Because she quickly realized that not everyone knows how to look at difference with respect.
She also remembers how something inside her slowly transformed: she began feeling the pain of other mothers and other children as if it were her own.

"We become a little like mothers to everyone," she says.
Protective. Attentive. Ready to help.
And, with effort, learning to forgive the ignorance of others too.

Today, Christian is twenty-three years old.
Rosario says it quietly, without grand gestures, with peaceful gratitude: God has been good to her.

Christian is respectful, loving, and affectionate.
Healthy. Happy.
He is funny, loves dancing, and fills his family's life with light.

Rosario does not romanticize the experience.
She knows there are far more complex conditions, heavier struggles, deeper pain. And from that awareness, she gives thanks.

Because her son, she says, has been a blessing.
Christian transformed her too.
He made her more patient.

He taught her to value every achievement, no matter how small it might seem.

He showed her another way of living:
without resentment, without bitterness, fully present in the moment.
"Now," she says,
"I am more like him than he is like me."

There is one image that still shines in her memory like a beacon.

During his recovery from surgery, she looked at her son's body covered in staples, tubes, and marks.

And silently, she prayed:
"Lord, let this pain be worth it.
Heal him.
Let everything be okay when he opens his eyes."

To other mothers, Rosario says this with tenderness and conviction:

Do not let sadness consume you.
Do not walk alone.

Seek help. Early therapies. Professionals. Support networks. Practice at home.
Teach without fear.

Do not limit your children, because you never truly know what they are capable of.

And above all:
do not believe fatalistic narratives.

They told her Christian would never hear, never speak, never accomplish anything.
They spoke in absolutes, as if his future had already been decided.

And if she could go back—if she could speak to the woman she was in that operating room—she wishes someone had simply told her:

"Don't be so afraid.
Your son is going to be okay.
He will learn.
One day he will say, 'Mom, thank you.'
He will love you.
He will bring you joy.
Just like any other baby."

Christian's story is not a perfect story.
Nor is it a miraculous exception.

It is the story of a promise made before she ever got to hold him.
A promise sustained through years of presence, patience, and love.

Not through denial of pain,
nor through impossible expectations,
but through a conscious and deeply human way of accompanying.

And when accompaniment is born from that place, the diagnosis no longer takes center stage.

And that—as this book gently reminds us—transforms the way life itself is lived.

A Story Without a Clear Name—But With Steady Love

In this testimony, the voice that guides us is that of a father who learned to hold on when love had to be stronger than loss.

There are lives that do not begin with a clear diagnosis,
but with confusion.

Karla's story began even before her birth, when her mother went to the doctor convinced that something was not right.

She was told it was not a pregnancy, but a "delay," and was given "something" to correct it.

No one explained much.
No one suspected what would later be discovered.
Months passed, and the delay did not resolve.
Then the truth came: she was pregnant.

The pregnancy unfolded without apparent complications,
as if the body knew how to remain silent until the very end.
Karla was born more than four decades ago, in a public hospital in Mexico.
At the time of birth, there were no clear explanations.

The doctors took the baby almost immediately and placed her in an incubator.

They said she was having difficulty breathing.
They spoke of oxygen, of observation, of waiting.
At first, they mentioned neonatal hypoxia.

Then they said they did not know exactly what she had.

A few days later, after several tests, she underwent an exchange transfusion—a medical procedure in which a large portion of a newborn's blood is replaced to treat serious complications at birth. She was also placed under blue light (phototherapy).

Her parents were told that with this, "she would be fine,"
but at the same time, they were prepared for what might come:
That there would likely be lasting effects.
That she would not develop like other children.

That she might have learning difficulties.
That her abilities might not go beyond those of a twelve- or thirteen-year-old.
Nothing was certain.
Nothing was fully explained.

Only the warnings remained…
and the love.
Karla returned home with her parents and siblings.
She was the fifth child.

From the very beginning, she was cared for, protected, and accompanied.
When school age came, the suspicions were confirmed:
Learning did not flow as it did for other children.

Her parents did not give up.
In addition to regular school, they enrolled her in special classes in the afternoons.

They sought support.
They insisted.
They waited.

Karla learned to read.
She learned basic math.
But her reasoning remained that of a child of about ten years old.
That limited her independence.

Adulthood, as the world defines it, was never a full possibility for her.
And even so… life continued.

Karla found things that made her shine.
She enjoys making bracelets to give away.
She does it with joy, with patience, with focus.

She also enjoys attending Zumba classes, which keep her active and bring her joy. Some neighbors trust her to accompany them and help care for young children, always under supervision.

Karla does it with affection, with attention,
with a kind of tenderness that cannot be taught.
She enjoys watching movies.
Going for walks.
Going to the cinema with her father.
Eating sweets. Laughing.
Being with her family.

Fifteen years ago, her mother passed away.
Since then, Karla has been in her father's care.

He is the one who walks beside her, who accompanies her in daily life, who understands her world and protects her without infantilizing her.

Her siblings and nieces and nephews are close.

They support. They hold.
They form a network around her.

Today, Karla is what many would call a "happy child."
And perhaps that is the most honest word.

Not because her life has been easy.
Not because there have not been losses, uncertainty, or exhaustion.
But because she was raised with love, patience, and presence.

Karla's story does not have a definitive diagnosis.
There is no clear label that fully explains her.
But there is something that was never in doubt:

Her right to be loved, cared for, and respected just as she is.
Over the years, her family learned that not everything is named,
that not everything is understood through medicine,
and that not every life needs a definition to have value.

Karla grew up surrounded by presence.
By patience.
By relationships that did not require her to change in order to belong.

And perhaps that is the deepest message her story leaves:

That even when medicine does not have all the answers,
love—when it is constant—can become guidance, support, and home.

Because beyond a diagnosis—or even in its absence—
there is a life that deserves to be seen with dignity.
And that, sometimes, is the only thing that truly matters.

The Gift Life Gave Me

Sometimes motherhood arrives by an unexpected path.
And yet, once it arrives… it stays forever.

At 35, I felt fulfilled.
I was happily married, my husband had just retired from the United States Army as an intelligence specialist, and at home we had three healthy children—ages 14, 12, and 8.
I was continuing to grow both professionally and personally.

I felt like a complete woman.

One day, my eight-year-old daughter said something that touched my heart: —"Mom… I want a little sister."
Honestly, I didn't want to expand our family. My husband did—he wanted "one more."

I shared this with a close friend, and she told me about Child Protective Services in El Paso (CPS).
"There are many children who need protection and care. You would be great candidates. Open your home as a foster family."

And that's how something I never imagined began.
We filled out the application. We completed training.
Our home was inspected. And then we waited for the call.

The first call: a fragile baby and a home that became both hospital and embrace. Our fourth daughter came straight from the hospital. I spent two weeks learning alongside doctors and nurses to make sure I could care for her.

She was a fragile baby, delicate, with health conditions I had never imagined facing.
And yet… she smiled.
She smiled as if hope lived in her face,
as if her very presence was saying: *"It's possible."*

At home, we were all happy.
It was chaos… but a meaningful chaos.
At four years old, we adopted her.
And as we walked alongside her life, I began to see the immense need among so many children who enter the system.

That led me to do more. I kept studying.
I took trainings—trauma, child development, behavior.
I thought I was prepared to care for children with special needs.

Then suddenly, my husband became ill.
Kidney failure—both kidneys—with no prior cause.
And I had to divide myself between my fragile daughter and my husband. That's when I understood something many mothers live:

Love does not always feel "beautiful."
Sometimes love is exhaustion.
Sometimes it is holding on without sleep.
Sometimes it is showing up when you yourself are falling apart.
And then, at 41, another call came.
CPS asked me to care for a newborn—born to a mother struggling with cocaine and alcohol.

I said no. Firmly.
I felt my hands were already full.

But the social worker insisted:
"Mrs. Victoria, I need you for this baby. I know you can help him."

And I… believed her.
I accepted, with one condition:
if my husband's health worsened, the baby would be removed from our home quickly.

And that's how Mike arrived. Six days old.
A beautiful baby, big for his age.

Mexican father, and a mother from the Ojibwe Band of Minnesota.
His features were confusing.
It wasn't clear whether it was a syndrome… or simply Indigenous traits.

I can't fully explain what I felt that day.
I only know that I felt he needed me.
Mike was quiet.
He hardly cried.
He followed me with his eyes when I spoke to him.
He didn't complain—not to eat, not during diaper changes.
Sometimes it seemed like he was just staring at the ceiling…
as if he were somewhere else.

Over time, I noticed delays.
He didn't roll over. He didn't sit.
He didn't crawl. I sought help.

Therapies began at home to strengthen his limbs.
I took him to a neurologist, and there I heard the first diagnosis—
explained in a way that left me full of questions:
"Inverted chromosome."

I didn't understand.
I asked him to explain.

He said something I still remember:
"Imagine a library. The book that belongs here… he has it on the other side."

And then a sentence that prepared me for what was coming:
"He will never see things the way you do. He will never reason the way you do. For him, everything will be harder and different. We have to wait and continue studying his development."

Mike didn't speak. He didn't laugh much.
He didn't show much.
But I… I understood him.

In the middle of everything, there was a legal battle over his custody.
The tribe and family members wanted to take him.
That was a deep blow. I already loved him.
He was already part of me.

More evaluations came.
Another diagnosis: intellectual disability.
I kept working with him, alongside my children.
He began to walk.
I thought: now speech will come. But it didn't.

Therapies began. Sign language.
I was clumsy learning… but I tried.
Mike was also diagnosed with vision problems and prescribed glasses. And I remember a moment that marked me deeply.

Someone close to us said something cruel:
"Poor baby… with that big head and prominent forehead, and now glasses? What else will happen to him? He looks even more abnormal."
I was deeply hurt.

I responded: "If you can be this cruel knowing him… what can we expect from others?"

Because that is another part of this journey:
You don't only fight diagnoses.
You also fight human ignorance.

After many court hearings, I learned that the tribe would no longer pursue custody. His grandparents loved him and visited, but living in Mexico, they didn't have the means to handle everything medically. They begged me to adopt him.

Around that time, a geneticist evaluated him and said something that also stayed with me:
"This child has features of several syndromes. I cannot diagnose him with a specific one. I need to see him again next year."

Then came the moment to decide.
I prayed. I spoke with my church.
I asked for guidance. My friend told me what I needed to hear:
"You will be able to do this."
My husband said:
"He's already been here two years. A change would affect him deeply. Let's move forward." And we did.

Mike was adopted.
It was a special day.
The whole family celebrated.

But life did not pause to honor our joy.
In 2003, when the Iraq conflict began, my second son was called to serve. Sadness filled the house. My husband fell into a deep depression. He withdrew. He disconnected.

At school, new challenges appeared.
ADHD diagnosis. Medication.
Constant frustration because Mike could not express himself the way he wanted.
Teachers reporting him for "behavior issues."
And me—again and again—advocating for him.

There were also asthma crises and hospitalizations.
We moved to Massachusetts seeking better medical care.
There, with intensive speech therapy, Mike began to speak.

Later came the autism diagnosis.
I already sensed it.
Changes in routine deeply affected him.
We lived between crises and exhaustion.
And I held on through prayer.

I celebrated small things: Two days without complaint calls.
Watching him dance *Thriller* in front of everyone. Immense pride.

We returned to El Paso.
On his first day at the new school, Mike didn't come home.
Calls. Police. Desperation.
He was eventually found at my mother's house—sweating, crying.
He didn't want to go back.

Later, he wrote a note saying he didn't want to live.
He was hospitalized. More tests.
A new diagnosis: bipolar disorder.
Another label. Another rebuilding.
But never defeat.

In high school, he lived intense years.

Strong emotions.
Setbacks. And then came graduation.

He wanted a diploma—not a certificate.
He studied two additional years to achieve it.
And he did.
After receiving it, he texted me: "Let's go."
I told him to wait for the parking lot to clear.
"No," he said. "I have my diploma now. Let's go eat."
That's Mike.

Today, he is part of a group where he feels he belongs.
He loves basketball.
He lives one day at a time.
If something doesn't go well, he says:
"It's okay. Another day will come."

If you ask me whether I would change anything, my answer is no.
Because when my son tells me:
"Mom… what would I be without you? You are the best mom."

I understand something profound:
I did not give him the gift of life.
Life gave me the gift of him.
And for that, I dedicate this poem to him, by an unknown author:

"I did not give you the gift of life,
but the love my heart feels for you
is as deep and real as if I had.
No… I did not give you the gift of life.
Life gave me the gift of you."

Diane: An Angel at Home

Not all journeys into motherhood begin gently.
Some begin too soon…
when we are not yet ready to let go.

Elizabeth remembers it this way.

During her pregnancy, everything seemed fine.
Until one day, she felt some discomfort.
She went to the doctor.
They told her Diane was ready to be born.

"But it's not time yet," she replied.
"Sometimes it happens this way," they told her.
And yes… it did.

Diane was born at seven months and three weeks.

In the delivery room, they tried for a natural delivery,
but Diane was tangled in the umbilical cord—wrapped twice around her neck.
They couldn't reposition her.
And then she was born.
Purple.
She had been deprived of oxygen to the brain.

From that moment on, her life began surrounded by wires, monitors…
and a painful distance: seeing her but not being able to hold her.
She remained in intensive care for about a month and a half,
alone in a room, connected to everything.

When it finally seemed they would be able to take her home…
she had a seizure.
And that "almost there" turned into more days in the hospital.

When she was finally discharged, another battle began.

During all that time, she had been fed through a tube.
So when she came home… Diane didn't know how to eat.
It wasn't a matter of willingness.
Her body simply didn't understand how.
They tried everything: breast milk, different formulas…
But nothing worked.
Her body rejected them.

Until they found one option she could tolerate: goat's milk.
And little by little, she began to move forward.

Diane had two seizures in total:
one in the hospital…
and another at home, when she was still very young.
After that, she never had another.

Over time, diagnoses began to emerge—
cerebral palsy… and, years later, autism.

Diane did not walk. She did not speak.
From a very young age, her body needed support just to stay upright.
They placed cushions at her sides because she had no stability.

Therapies began…
as well as the use of braces, since her legs turned inward.
The process was long.
At first, she didn't walk.

Then she began to move by dragging her feet… always with support.
Her shoes didn't last even a month.
With time—and a great deal of work—
she took her first steps around the age of five.

Therapies—physical, occupational, and speech—
were part of her life for years.
And thanks to them, she continued to make steady progress.

She also showed echolalia… repeating everything.
But over time, with the right support, this improved.

At 14, Diane underwent a complex surgery.
Her bones were cut, rotated, and rods were inserted to correct the position of her legs.
After that came the wheelchair.
A year later, the rods were removed…
and the change was significant.

Today, Diane can walk on her own.
Not completely.
She still needs support going downstairs,
and requires constant supervision to prevent falls, as she has had several.
That is why Elizabeth is always nearby… watching every step.

But looking back, the progress is undeniable.

After that surgery, she also had a procedure on the ligaments behind her knees.
And that was when the family made an important decision:
no more surgeries.

They were very painful for Diane.
And they felt they had gone as far as they should with her body.

Therapies continued for years,
until finally, with all the progress she had made,
the specialists explained something clearly:
Diane's brain does not properly send signals to her legs.

And with that understanding…
came acceptance.
Not a resigned acceptance,
but a conscious one.

Diane is a child of challenges.

She has never given up.
She always tries.
Always.

Elizabeth became her teacher.
At home, she created a classroom-like space:
a board, books, materials…
and there, among many things, she taught Diane to read in Spanish.
Diane reads very well.
They have always taken her everywhere:
therapies, activities, events…
And if there is a place where she cannot be,
they simply don't go.
Her place is with her family.

Her education took place in public schools,
where she received special education services,
and she always had teachers who supported her.

They have tried to give her as normal a life as possible:
with discipline, with structure… and with love.

Diane is very sensitive.
And that has also been an important part of her care.
They try to avoid making her cry,
because what she feels… she carries for a long time.

When Elizabeth received the autism diagnosis,
she was asked how she felt.
Her answer was simple:

"Good… because she will receive more services."
Because diagnoses do not change love.

The hardest part has not been Diane.
It has been people.

Elizabeth never forgets one moment:
Diane was about three years old.
While playing at a pizza place, Elizabeth was feeding her with a training cup.
A woman commented:
"She's so big… and you're still feeding her like that."
She didn't know Diane couldn't hold the cup.

That day, Elizabeth understood something she never questioned again:
it doesn't matter what people think.
As long as she knows she is doing the best for her daughter… that is enough.

Since then, she takes Diane everywhere.
Without shame. Without explanations.
And if they are not welcomed somewhere, they simply don't return.

Because people are never satisfied.
If you correct, they criticize.
If you don't, they criticize too.
So she chose to focus on what matters… and keep going.

To mothers who are just beginning, Elizabeth would say:
first—accept.

Without acceptance, there is no path.

And also something practical, but meaningful:
keep your children clean, well-dressed, well cared for.
It changes the way the world perceives them.

But beyond that…
what truly defines Diane is not how she looks.
It is who she is.

Diane loves puzzles.
She can spend hours putting them together.

At night, mother and daughter lie on the floor…
and work on them side by side.
She enjoys choosing her shoes,
making small decisions,
doing for herself what she has learned with so much effort.

She cannot bathe completely on her own,
but she dresses herself, brushes her hair, brushes her teeth…
She is organized.
She is clean.

And as part of her path toward independence,
they have also adapted to other needs.

Diane has experienced digestive issues,
and to help her gain control and autonomy, they implemented a simple but effective system: a calendar in the bathroom, which they call the "poop calendar."
There, she tracks each time she goes.

Because independence… is also something that is taught.

At school, Diane lived meaningful experiences.
She was crowned queen at her high school.

She also graduated in the top ten of her class,
and that day, she received a trophy in recognition of all her effort…
but for her family, the real recognition was everything she had overcome to get there.

She always participated.
She was always included.
And that, too, was a decision:
to give her the opportunity to fully live her experiences.

There is still a path ahead.
Not everything is written.

But today, Elizabeth is certain of something:
in a world filled with anger, resentment, and indifference…
in her home, there is someone who knows none of that.

Diane does not know rejection.
She does not know malice.
She only knows how to love.

She is genuine.
She is authentic.
She is kind.

And for that…
Elizabeth is certain of something that needs no explanation:
she has an angel at home.

The Yellow Brick Road We Didn't Choose

(But Walked Anyway)

Some stories do not need explanation,
because they already carry their truth within them.

They are not trying to convince, teach, or prove anything.
They simply exist. And in existing, they accompany.

This is one of those stories.
Adriana arrived on this path in an unconventional way.
Her son Rodrigo did not come into her life following the expected order.

He was not born from her body,
but he was born from a choice that has sustained her for a lifetime:
love. A love that goes beyond blood, and far beyond diagnosis.

There is no idealized mother here, no perfect family.
There is longing, loss, waiting, surprise, honesty.
There is fear, exhaustion, questions that do not always find answers.

And there is something even deeper:
a way of loving that transforms over time.

A mother who learned—sometimes by force, sometimes with tenderness—
that not everything can be controlled,
that not everything can be understood,
and that not everything needs to be "fixed" to have value.

Reading this story is an invitation:

to walk, even for a few pages,
that yellow brick road that was not always smooth,
but was always meaningful.

This is Rodrigo's story… told through his mother's eyes:

It can't be!
We wanted children so much, and we couldn't have them.
So many tests, so many treatments, so many attempts… and nothing.

It can't be!
I finally became pregnant—only for the hope to last three months.
We lost the baby. What grief. What despair.
We decided to adopt, and after nine months, we did.
We were filled with joy and hope.

It can't be!
God gave us a beautiful baby boy,
and He was so good to us that seven months later—after a normal pregnancy—
He also blessed us with a precious baby girl who completed the family we had longed for.

Six years later:
"Your son is not normal and never will be.
He has autism and attention deficit hyperactivity disorder."

It can't be!
"You will have to adapt your entire world to your son's needs,
because he will never be able to adapt to the world."

Fear. Uncertainty. Anguish.
Courses, conferences, books, neurologists, tests, doctors.

Years of therapy and special education.
And still… everything felt the same.
So hard to accept.

A daughter—intelligent, loving, joyful, hardworking, responsible, independent, deeply committed to her community.
Always looking to help the most vulnerable.
Always supporting those with disabilities.
Always caring for her brother. Always loving him deeply.

A son—kind, responsible, patient, positive, empathetic, gentle, affectionate, deeply sensitive to human suffering.

He never complains.
He never speaks badly of anyone.
He has a pure heart.
He is passionate about film, history, travel, and food.

And yet, perfection exists only in a mother's heart,
and love can sometimes blind us. Reality is different.

Daily life shows us that the idea of thinking our children are "little angels" simply because they are special… is just that:
a fantasy.

My son also has flaws.
He also controls us when we give in to his vulnerability.
It hurts to see his limitations, his obsessions, his struggles.
And to be completely honest,
there are times when his constant presence feels overwhelming.

Because he doesn't have friends who invite him to parties,
to go out, to have fun, to grab a drink, to meet girls.

He cannot go shopping on his own.
He cannot find a job by himself.
He cannot travel alone or go on trips.

His life depends on our support and companionship.
His youth is passing among busy and tired adults.
And ours is shaped around him too,
around the responsibility of making his life as full as possible.

We are bound for life.

And our time—as individuals, as a couple, as a marriage—
is always postponed…
for when someone can care for him,
or when an activity comes up where he can participate on his own.

And we accept it—with love and with surrender.
Because seeing him happy and fulfilled is our priority.
Because we love him.

How could I ever forget that Monday, January 11, 2001—
the day our lives changed with a call from the Family Development
Office (DIF for Desarrollo Integral de la Familia),
telling us they had our son and we could go meet him?

The very next day, we found out… I was pregnant.

We never imagined that in just two days
we would begin such a profound journey—
and that those two little lives would draw for us a yellow brick road:
sometimes rocky, sometimes smooth and light.

Sometimes I feel like the lion, asking for courage
to face the great challenge of raising a son so different—

a son the world often does not understand,
and does not care to understand,
let alone support or accept.

Other times, I feel like the scarecrow,
needing a brilliant mind
to guide him toward the fulfillment he longs for—
a fulfillment society often denies him.

And sometimes, I feel like the tin man,
longing for a heart capable of returning
the immense love my son gives me every day—
quietly, without show, without pride, without malice.

In the end, I am simply Dorothy—
walking the road without knowing what lies ahead,
but never turning back.
Continuing forward with uncertainty, but with tireless strength,
seeking a place for my son in a world
that so often chooses to ignore him.

Twenty-four years later, I still wonder why God chose us—ordinary parents— to care for someone extraordinary.
There are no words, actions, thoughts, or feelings
enough to express gratitude
for the privilege and blessing of being part of His perfect plan
and being gifted with two incredible children.

I would love to say that I have learned all of my son's virtues.
That I am now more patient, more tolerant.
That I have learned to live more humbly, as he does—
to see the good in every situation and every person, as he does.
But I would be arrogant and dishonest if I said that.

Because it's not true.
I look at my son and admire him because he is still like a child.
At 25, he is simple, humble, content, respectful, thoughtful.
And as I always say:
if we were all like him, this world would be very different.

It would be a better world.
Yes, I know it sounds like a cliché… but it is the truest one I know.

And yet, I am still the same person I have always been—
with all my flaws.
And although I have tried thousands of times to be more like Rodrigo, I still haven't achieved it.

I admire him deeply
and I always pray that God continues to bless us with this wonderful and extraordinary son.
He is an example to us.
The miracle of having him has brought me great joy.
And my gratitude to God has helped me transform fear into joy,
and uncertainty into hope.

To you, who are just beginning…
I hope that your journey as a mother—
whatever color it may be—
will also fill you with a little bit of everything.
And that in the end, you find the peace that only pure, steady love for your child can bring.

Blessings.
—Adriana

The yellow brick road does not end here…
it simply changes its scenery.

Every Day is a Gift

Rocío was 21years old when she became a mother for the first time.

Her pregnancy had been uneventful, like so many others: regular checkups, quiet excitement, small plans forming almost without noticing.
Nothing suggested that the moment of birth would change her life forever.

Phillip's birth was not what she had imagined.
Instead of the cry that announces a new arrival, there was rushed movement, overlapping voices, doctors and nurses speaking to one another in a language she could not fully understand. Everything happened quickly and felt confusing. Too fast.

Phillip was taken away immediately.
Rocío barely had a chance to see him.
She couldn't hold him freely in her arms.
His tiny body was surrounded by machines, tubes, and unfamiliar sounds.

Hours later — when fear had already settled in — someone tried to explain what was happening.
They told her that her baby had been born with microcephaly, meaning his head was smaller than expected for his body.
He had low birth weight and was experiencing seizures.

They spoke of global developmental delays, intellectual disability, and multiple complications if he survived — including respiratory, hearing, feeding, and mobility challenges.

They talked about very limited chances of survival, without offering

a clear explanation of why this had happened.
They painted a frightening future, filled with limitations and warnings of medical risks.

Rocío did not understand everything.
But she understood enough to know that nothing would ever be the same.

And in the middle of that chaos, there was one thing she was certain of: she was not going to let go of her son. And she didn't.
With the unconditional support of her mother, she began a path she did not choose but decided to walk with love.

Therapies, appointments, medical instructions, forced learning.
Day after day, step by step.

Today, Phillip is fifteen years old.
Against every prognosis that said he would not live beyond his first year, Phillip is still here.
He attends ninth grade in a special education program, where he shares space with other young people his age.

He does not speak and walks with difficulty,
but he communicates through basic signs.
He smiles when something — or someone — brings him joy.
He recognizes, responds, feels.

Phillip takes his place in the world at his own pace.

His family surrounds him with love: his mother, his grandmother, and his two younger siblings.

They all agree on something simple and profound: Phillip brought joy into their lives.

Rocío works, and her mother — Phillip's grandmother — has taken on a central role in his daily care.

She is the one who gets him ready for school, who picks him up, who takes him to his physical, occupational, and speech therapies.

It is a quiet network of love that sustains everyday life.

Phillip's grandmother often says something that captures these fifteen years of struggle and hope:

"Every day is a gift."

Because when Phillip was born, they were told he would not live past his first year.

And yet, at fifteen, he is still learning, still trying, still developing in his own way.

Rocío and her mother share this story for what it is:
a real life shaped by fear, uncertainty, exhaustion…
and also by a strength born from the deepest kind of love.
Their story does not seek answers. It seeks companionship.

To remind us that, even when everything seems lost,
life can find its way through in unexpected ways.

That prognoses do not have the final word.

And that there are stories which, without promising easy endings, teach us that continuing… is also a way of loving.

I Only Cried for One Night

When a mother looks back after so many years, some memories still hurt, and others transform into gratitude.

Elida shares both—pain and gratitude intertwined—even from before Ángel left the hospital.

She does not tell her story from fear.
She tells it from the calm that can only come after facing the unimaginable.

Her motherhood began among operating rooms, tubes, and decisions no manual teaches you how to make.

Today, Ángel is a joyful, respectful young man, full of light.
But getting here was a long, difficult, and deeply human road.

This is her voice:

Ángel was born on June 8, 1998, by C-section.
I had just had surgery when, only a few hours after he was born, he was transferred to the Children's Hospital.

When they tried to insert a tube through his throat,
they realized it wouldn't pass.
He had a problem in his esophagus.
He was born with esophageal atresia.

I stayed at the hospital where I gave birth… but only for a few hours. I signed myself out against medical advice and left on my own responsibility.
I could not stay in a bed while my son was in another hospital.

No one mentioned Down syndrome.

But when I finally saw him, I knew.
I told my husband, "Ángel has Down syndrome."
The doctor confirmed it—and added something more:
that he would not see, that he would not walk, that he would not recognize us.

That night, I cried.
Only that night.

Because while I was crying,
he was fighting to breathe.
And I understood that I could not stay in fear.

At just twelve hours old, he went into surgery to reconnect his esophagus.
During that process, they discovered he also had two holes in his heart.
At first, he was fed through a nasogastric tube.

But after a month to a month and a half, the doctors said they could not continue that way—the tubes through his nose were beginning to affect his lungs. It was dangerous.

So they placed a gastric tube directly into his stomach.
I learned how to clean it, disinfect it, and use a machine to feed him drop by drop, like an IV.

It wasn't feeding him.
It was sustaining him minute by minute.
But Ángel did not tolerate milk well that way.
Because of the complications, they changed the system to a tube

that went directly into his stomach—a G-tube.

A month later, they replaced it with one that goes into the small intestine, the duodenum—a J-tube—so he could absorb nutrients better.
At that point, Ángel was barely two and a half months old…
and he had already gone through multiple surgeries:
his esophagus, the placement of the gastric tube, the change to the intestinal tube… and still ahead of him was the biggest one: open-heart surgery.

Medication was not working to close the second hole.
He became agitated easily. We had to keep him almost completely still so he wouldn't become distressed.

Watching such a small baby go through open-heart surgery is something that never leaves you.
I saw him full of tubes, his chest open…
and Down syndrome was the last thing on my mind.
What mattered was that he lived.
When he began to stabilize from the heart surgery, my next goal became clear: to teach him how to feed.

It didn't happen overnight.
They had told me he couldn't—that he didn't have the strength.
But when the cardiologist gave me the green light, I started little by little.

With surgical gloves, I stimulated his palate with my finger.
He didn't know what his mouth was for.
We started with half an ounce, then one, then two…
with a tiny bottle, with the smallest nipple.

It took days of persistence. And months of patience.

Until he was able to drink eight full ounces.
And then another conflict began.

At the hospital, they insisted I should continue feeding him through the gastric tube.
I refused.
I could see that he was able to eat by mouth.
The tube became infected.
They scolded me in the emergency room.

They told me that if they removed the tube and something went wrong, there would be no way to place it again.
I insisted.
They made me sign documents taking full responsibility for anything that might happen.

I signed.

It wasn't irresponsibility.
It was conviction.
I saw my son eating.
And that tube made him suffer—he would pull at it, remove it, bleed.
When they finally removed it, I felt an enormous victory.

But the esophageal surgery had left an internal scar.
Even the smallest piece of food would get stuck.
He would choke.
We went to the emergency room constantly.

Sometimes we spent the night sitting against a wall,
him between my legs, not laying him down,
waiting for him to stop drooling.

That was the sign that he had finally swallowed what was stuck.
In the middle of all this, I had no time to process the diagnosis.

I cried one night.
After that, I dedicated myself to fighting.
Because Down syndrome was the least important thing.

When it seemed like the most intense medical phase was ending…
another surprise came: leukemia.
Bruises that wouldn't go away.
Extreme fatigue. Yellowish skin.
A swollen abdomen. He stopped eating.
He was hospitalized.
And we spent a year and two months practically living there.

The chemotherapy was devastating.
His veins became infected.
At one point, they had to administer chemo through a vein in his head because there were no other access points left.

We slept sitting up—sometimes for up to 72 hours at a time.
I never let him go.
Over time, the doctors noticed that my skin was peeling.
They explained that, from being in such constant contact, I was also absorbing residues from the treatment.

They asked me to lay him down during the infusions to protect myself. It wasn't easy to let him go.

The hospital chemotherapy ended.
Then outpatient treatment.
Then medication.
He went into remission.
He did not relapse.

But then came fainting episodes.
Cardiac aftereffects from the chemotherapy appeared.
He went into surgery once again.
They placed a pacemaker in his abdomen because there was not enough muscle in his arm to place it there.

More hospital. More surgeries. More monitoring.

Once he recovered, we moved to El Paso on medical advice.
The climate and pollution in Los Angeles were not good for him.
They recommended a dry climate.

And when the medical battles began to stabilize…
another one began: school.
Fighting for inclusion.
Demanding services.
Seeking legal support.

Ángel went through difficult behavioral stages:
biting, screaming, crying.
Therapies were essential.

I was there the whole time.
I always say I graduated with him.
I volunteered throughout his middle school and high school years.
I needed to be there—to stay close, to stay aware.
And all that effort was worth it.

He became the first student with Down syndrome at his school to be admitted into ROTC (Reserve Officers' Training Corps), a leadership program inspired by military training.

He was recognized at graduation.

He learned to read. To write.
To connect with others.
Ángel no longer gives me difficulties.
He is a respectful, kind, loving young man.

When we go out, I feel at peace.
I'm not afraid of a public scene.
That, for me, is peace.

But there is something that still hurts.
My daughter was six years old when Ángel was born.

I spent a year and two months in the hospital.
I had no consistent support, no family nearby.
She stayed with whoever could take care of her.

I believed she was fine. But she wasn't always.
Today, she is an adult.
And I know she still carries what she lived through in her childhood.

I am proud of everything I achieved with Ángel.
But if I could go back in time,
the first thing I would do
is not neglect my daughter.
I don't know how I would have done it…
but I would have found a way.

To all mothers who are just beginning this journey,
this is my most sincere advice:
Do not forget your neurotypical children
because of your neurodivergent child's condition.

Because they are living the story too.
Only—many times—in silence.

When Accompanying Also Means Building a Path

Although every diagnosis is different, the emotions we experience as mothers are universal.

Mariquel opens her heart here to share how she has lived the journey of autism in her life, with the hope that her voice may accompany other women who are feeling the same today.

The story you are about to read belongs to Giselle, her daughter.

The journey began with her diagnosis—a moment that completely transformed her life and that of her family.

Mariquel chose to share her experience with courage,
not as a formula or a perfect story,
but as a testimony of love, struggle, and hope.

When Giselle was born, nothing seemed out of the ordinary.

She was a cheerful, social baby,
with development that, to everyone's eyes, appeared typical.
She babbled, ate well, responded to touch, played.

There were no clear signs that anything was wrong.
No alarms.

It was around eighteen months that Mariquel began to notice changes. They did not come suddenly.
It was more of a shift in behavior:
Giselle began to withdraw, to show anxiety and irritability, to lose interest in interaction.

Her temperament changed.
She became more reserved.

She would spend long periods arranging objects, stacking cans and dishes, repeating patterns that no one at the time could explain.

The diagnosis came around the age of two: autism.

And with it, confusion. Fear.
Questions without answers.
Mariquel remembers how little was known about the condition at the time,
how limited access to information was,
and how the film *Rain Man* was one of the few references she had.

She also remembers the urgent need to understand.
One of the moments that marked her most
was when she took Giselle to kindergarten and began explaining her condition and the diagnosis the doctor had given her.

The teacher's first response was a question that today might seem unthinkable, but at the time was common:
"What is autism?"

That moment made something painfully clear:
she would not only have to accompany her daughter—
she would also have to educate the world around her.

Mariquel did not stop.
She sought guidance.
She read.
She asked.
She knocked on doors.

She connected with associations and support groups.
Giselle was diagnosed at a time when autism was poorly understood and even less recognized in girls.

There were no major organizations,
no accessible information on social media,
no clear paths.

So Mariquel did what so many mothers do:
she searched tirelessly.

She even traveled outside her city to explore therapeutic options, such as Applied Behavior Analysis (ABA) therapy in Chihuahua, Mexico, at a time when it was not yet widely known.

She tried dietary changes and everything that was suggested to her.

She searched for possibilities, gathered tools,
looked for answers that might help her daughter develop.

For years, life revolved around that search.

Until, little by little, something began to take shape within her:
the certainty that not all forms of support mean doing more.

Over time, Mariquel came to understand something essential:
there is no single correct way to accompany.

That love is also expressed through the search—
but not every search requires constant urgency.

That there are moments to try everything…
and moments to pause and look more calmly.

That there is also a way of accompanying through presence.
Through stability.
Through simply being.

Mariquel then chose to shift her approach.
Not to abandon support, but to balance it.

After years of therapies, travel, and constant effort, she made a deep and conscious decision:
to prioritize quality time.

To be present.

Not only for Giselle, but also for her other daughter.

To choose presence over urgency.
Connection over constant pressure.

Giselle grew up in an environment of clear routines and stable structures, where she feels safe.

She is nonverbal and requires ongoing support.
Mariquel does not go anywhere without her.

Giselle is her constant companion, her daily presence, her responsibility, and her deepest bond.
Giselle does not live independently,
but that does not define her value or limit what she has achieved.

Because her path is full of real progress.

She graduated from high school.
She takes piano lessons.

She deeply enjoys music, movies, and sports.
She finds pleasure and calm in what is familiar and meaningful to her.

Her life does not follow traditional measures of success,
but it is full of abilities, learning, and moments that reflect genuine growth.

Through her experience as a mother,
Mariquel also began to look beyond her own story.

Over time, as she realized that many families faced the same uncertainty when their children grew up and left the school system, she began to seek options where none existed.

She did this not only for Giselle,
but for many others who needed a place where they could be seen and valued.

She began to guide other parents,
to create spaces and activities that offered more than waiting and isolation:
places where young adults with different disabilities could connect, develop, feel included, and supported.

Not as a formal project,
but as an urgent need born from love for her daughter
and the desire that no family should face that emptiness alone.

The story of Mariquel and Giselle is not a story of miracles or universal formulas.

It is a story of conscious choices.

Of intense searching—and necessary pauses.
Of understanding that there is no single correct way to accompany.

Sometimes accompanying means pushing forward.
Other times, it means holding steady.
And sometimes, it simply means staying.

This is a story where love was not measured by independence achieved,
but by dignity preserved.

Where progress was not compared,
but honored in its rightful measure.
And where life, just as it is, was embraced with respect.
Because beyond the diagnosis,
Giselle is not a label or a prognosis.

She is a young woman with abilities, preferences, sensitivity, and presence.

This story—like so many others—reminds us
that accompanying can also be a profound act of loyalty,
consistency, and love that does not give up.

For Mariquel, what began as a personal search gradually became, without her even realizing it, a meeting point for many others.

Perhaps that is one of the deepest meanings of these stories:

to transform pain into connection,
to step into the world with what has been lived,
and to turn it into light for other families who are just beginning.

Before We Continue…

The stories you have just read are more than just testimonies: they are pieces of life offered with a love that overflows any page. Each one is different, but all are born from the same place: the unbreakable love for a child.

Listening to these voices is a reminder that none of us is alone. That this kind of motherhood is not an individual destination, but a community that grows stronger when someone dares to share what they are living.

Because each testimony is more than a story: it is a light, an embrace, an invitation to keep moving forward.

Today, I want to deeply thank every mother and every father who opened their souls in this chapter.
Each person who spoke here carried their pain, their faith, their exhaustion, and their hope… and still chose to share it.
That is not just an act of courage.
That is an act of generosity.

They left behind the fear of judgment to offer companionship to those who may just be beginning this journey, or to those walking it in solitude. Their stories do not seek applause: they seek to extend a hand, offer hope, and remind us that this struggle has meaning.

Each story comes from a different place.

Autism. Down syndrome. Complex genetic conditions. Accidents. Illnesses. Invisible disabilities. Adoption stories that arrived as an unexpected miracle. Different diagnoses.

Different paths, yes… but the same heartbeat: that of a mother who loves to the core and who, even while trembling, keeps moving forward.

Reading them is remembering that this path was never a solitary one.

While you are navigating your fears,
there is another mother staying awake in an emergency room;
another filling out forms;
another searching for a specialist;
another celebrating a small milestone with tears in her eyes;
and another looking for a space where her child can simply be.

All different.
All united by something that cannot be described, only felt.

These voices teach us that sharing is not exposing weakness,
but illuminating the path for someone else.
That when a mother dares to tell her truth,
she opens a crack in the darkness
through which another can look and think:
"I am not the only one."

These testimonies inspire us to continue defending what we love and remind us of a truth we must not forget: our children are not less because of their differences.

They are whole human beings,
with dignity, worth, and the right to belong.
They deserve a world that sees them with respect,
that includes them, and that opens doors for them.

To all of them: thank you.

Thank you for lending us your voice.
Thank you for naming what many remain silent about.
Thank you for trusting these pages and allowing your story to echo in other lives.

Thank you for reminding us that this kind of motherhood
is not a solitary burden,
but an invisible network that grows stronger
with every honest word.

And to every child who inspires these stories…
Thank you.

Thank you for teaching us to see life from a different place.
Thank you for reminding us that love
is not measured in standards,
or diagnoses,
or prognoses.

Because, even if the path is different,
every day with you is worth more than any difficulty.

Before we continue, let us honor these voices.
Let their words settle into our hearts.
Let us breathe with them.
Walk with them.

Because what comes next will continue building on this truth: we are not alone, and we never will be.

My Story: Two Diagnoses, One Love

I am Cruz Elena.
I am the mother of two children: first a daughter, then a son.

They came into this world with completely different stories but wrapped in the same love.
My daughter was my little piece of heaven.
My son came to be my little piece of life.

Neither of them came to teach me what I would later learn.
Both led me down paths I never imagined walking.

Two diagnoses.
Two processes.
Two griefs that are not alike.
Two rebirths that did not happen at the same time or in the same way.

And one certainty that runs through everything:
the love for my children transformed me forever.

When the diagnosis came with my son

The first diagnosis of my life did not arrive as a sudden blow.
It was more like a puzzle that took me years to understand.

My son walked late.
He spoke late.
He avoided eye contact.
He rejected certain foods.
He covered his ears at sounds that others barely noticed.

Today, I recognize those signs.
Back then, they deeply confused me.
In those years, I knew nothing about neurodiversity.
I only knew what I had heard all my life:

"You've spoiled him too much."
"He's lazy."
"It's just a phase, boys develop slower."
"You're not setting limits."

And without realizing it, I began repeating the same things to myself, trying to convince myself that everything was fine and that it was just a matter of time and more discipline.

I remember his second-grade teacher calling me over and over again to say that he was not using his time wisely, that he was always daydreaming, that he was lazy.

I remember scolding him in ways that still hurt my soul today. Moments when I thought he was challenging me, when in reality he was struggling to survive in a world that was too loud, too fast, and too demanding for him.

When I heard the words attention deficit and level 1 autism, something inside me broke.

First came disbelief.
Then, as I began putting the pieces together, acceptance arrived.

I felt relief at finally understanding him.
But also a deep pain for everything I myself had failed to see.

That is where our true story began.

Therapies several times a week.
Clear routines. Visual schedules all over the house.
Structured environments.
Medication, despite the fear and the horror stories I had heard.
Everything that could give him the opportunity to have a better quality of life.

I learned to anticipate. To translate the world for him.
To hold him. But above all, I learned to see him again.

Without judgment. Without outside expectations.
With new eyes.

I understood that he never wanted to challenge me or break rules.

I learned that my son is not less or more.
He is different.

I learned to give him step-by-step instructions instead of demanding everything at once.
To offer him food with patience, allowing him to explore without pressure.

To enjoy his deep interest in dinosaurs and jungle animals, listening to detailed explanations that reminded me that his mind works differently… different from most, but not in an inferior way.

It has not been easy.
Fear still appears.
Guilt does too.

Because level 1 autism—what many call "mild"—comes with an invisible cost.

The constant pressure to fit in.
The anxiety that is not always visible.
The emotional exhaustion of a child who spends the day adapting to a world that is not designed for the way he feels.

Today, in adolescence, my son is finding his balance.

Music, Legos, and predictable spaces give him security.

He knows that his brain works differently.
And although he has made great progress, emotionally it is still difficult to let go of labels and others' expectations.
He has few friends, yes.
But he has an inner world full of sensitivity, creativity, and a deep kindness.

And I have learned that life at his pace is also a full life.
Not perfect. Not easy.
But deeply human.

My daughter's story: between what I dreamed… and what I learned to love

My daughter, my firstborn, had a completely typical development.

She was strong. Sociable.
Confident. Full of plans.

I never imagined that a mosquito bite would split our lives in two.

Neuroinvasive West Nile virus.
Meningoencephalitis.
Coma.

The worst prognoses.
One month in intensive care.
Constantly waiting for the worst.

And then, months of hospitalization, fighting to relearn absolutely everything.

When she woke up, she was breathing on her own.
She could do nothing else. But that alone was already a miracle.

At fifteen, she became like a baby again.

She could not hold her head up.
There was no eye contact.
She could not walk. She could not speak. She could not eat.

The prognoses were devastating:

that she would not survive,
that she would not leave the hospital,
that she would never speak again,
that she would not walk,
that she would not even recognize us.

But my daughter held on to life.
And life, sometimes, holds on with a strength that no diagnosis can contain.

With intensive therapies, specialists, daily work, and a faith I cannot explain, she began to return.

First, she lifted her head.
Then she communicated with her eyes.
Then she moved her hand.

She walked again.
She relearned how to write.

Months later—months that felt like centuries—she spoke again.

Her life began again.
So did ours.

Today, years later, she is still in therapy.

She has cognitive sequelae, yes.
She depends on me for many things.

She attends school. She was accepted into a university program for young people with disabilities.
She fights every day for her independence, step by step, at her own pace.

Medically, her story is a miracle.
But daily life is much more complex.

The dream of full independence faded.
Vulnerability is constant.

My daughter lives in that in-between space that is so difficult to explain:
she does not have a severe and visible disability,
but she also does not have the protection the world offers to those who clearly need it.

"She looks normal," they say.
But her mind is innocent, transparent, trusting—like that of a young child.

And that makes her deeply vulnerable.
Keeping her safe is one of the greatest challenges of my life.

What I learned between the two diagnoses

Sometimes people ask me which story was more difficult.

And today… I no longer try to answer that.

Because it is not about which one hurt more.
It is about everything that changed.

One story arrived slowly,
like a puzzle I took time to understand.

The other came without warning,
splitting my life in two.

Two different paths.
Two forms of grief.
Two ways of beginning again.

But deep down…
the same movement.

Rebuilding myself.
Learning again.
Holding on… even when I did not know how.

Because when a diagnosis arrives—whatever it may be—
life is never the same again.

Plans change.

Dreams rearrange.
The future stops being something certain…
and becomes something that is built, day by day.

And along the way…

fear appears.
Guilt too.
Exhaustion settles in places no one sees.

It does not matter how the diagnosis came,
or how visible it is.

All the mothers who walk this path
have felt that weight…
and also that strength that lifts us again.

But there is something that does not change.

Love.

And with it…
the way a mother stays.
Learns.
Adapts.
And rises again, as many times as needed.

My children do not live life the way I imagined.
And I… am not the mother I thought I would be.

I am someone else.

Someone who learned to see beyond expectations.

To celebrate what once seemed small.
To find meaning even in uncertainty.

This is not the story I planned.
But it is the story I love.

Because in the end…
these were not two separate stories.

They were two different diagnoses…
and one same love.

And here we are.

Walking.
Learning.
Loving.

Beyond the diagnosis.

Together.

6.

The Beginning of a New Path

"Sometimes a new path begins while the soul is still trembling…

but chooses to take one more step."

When Life Forces You to Begin Again

A diagnosis is an earthquake.
It does not matter whether you had sensed it for some time or if it took you by surprise; no mother is ever truly prepared to hear words that forever change a child's life… and our own.

In those first days, everything feels different.
Breathing hurts. Thinking is frightening.
The heart seems to move faster than the mind, and questions pile up without giving us time to process them.
The future becomes a dense fog where it is hard to see even the next step.

And yet, it is precisely in that chaos—in the mix of fear, shock, love, and confusion—that a completely new path begins.
A path we did not choose. One we never imagined.
And one that demands a strength we do not yet know we have.

The first days often feel like a free fall: too much information, too many decisions, too many emotions all at once.
And yet, little by little, almost without noticing, we begin to discover small certainties that help us stay on our feet: a look from our child, a kind word from a professional, an unexpected hug, a night of rest after so many without sleep.

This chapter does not aim to give you perfect solutions, because they do not exist. It will not tell you how to stop feeling afraid, because that would be unfair. It does not promise that everything will be easy, because you and I both know it is not.
But it does want to be an embrace. A gentle pause before continuing.
A guide to remind you that, even if the world seems to have

completely changed, you do not have to walk this path alone.
Here you will find practical steps, simple ideas, and emotional tools that can support you as you adjust to this new life—not from pressure, but from humanity.

It is not about learning everything immediately or becoming an expert overnight. No one can do that.
It is about moving forward at your own pace.
Listening to your heart. Asking for help without shame.
Trusting that each day will teach you something new about your child… and about yourself.

Because, although a diagnosis marks a before and an after, it also opens an unexpected path: one of strengthened love, resilience that emerges without warning, and the ability—sometimes trembling, but real—to begin again.

Perhaps that is why, even in the midst of pain, many people discover something they did not imagine at the beginning: that suffering does not always destroy the meaning of life; sometimes, it transforms it.

Psychiatrist Viktor Frankl, who survived the concentration camps during World War II, wrote that even in the most difficult circumstances, human beings retain the possibility of finding meaning to move forward.
We may not always choose what happens to us, but we can discover the meaning we give to what we live.
And when that happens, little by little, almost without realizing it, you begin to see that you are not alone.
That you never were.

Remember this. Sometimes, all it takes is one more step
to find companionship along the way.

Discovering Your Strength… One Day at a Time

The first days after a diagnosis are a mix of fear, disbelief, and a kind of pain that is hard to name because it is unfamiliar.
It is not just sadness—it is confusion, uncertainty, helplessness.
It is the fear of not knowing how to care for the life you love most in a place you do not know.

The mind rushes into the future before you can stop it:
What will happen to my child?
What will become of their life?
How am I going to do this?
Will I be able to?
What if I do not do it right?

And it is natural for it to do so.
Love always tries to move ahead in order to protect.
But the truth is that trying to think about everything at once only feeds the anxiety.
No one can walk an entire path while still trembling from the impact of the first step.

In those moments, the healthiest thing is to return to the present.
One day at a time.
One hour at a time, if necessary.

Life is not lived in predictions.
It is lived in small, everyday acts.
It is not lived in years—it is lived in days, in moments, in what you are able to hold today.

And even though today may hurt, it is also true that hope grows in small steps.

Today, even breathing may feel heavy.
Tomorrow, it may feel a little lighter.

Allow yourself to release the pressure.
Letting go of self-judgment is, many times, the first act of care.
From there, the heart begins—little by little—to find new ways to hold itself.

Allow yourself to feel.
Crying does not make you weak; it releases you.
Sadness does not make you a bad mother; it makes you human and reminds you how deeply you love. Anger, frustration, confusion… all are valid emotions that need space.

You do not have to deny them.
You do not have to hide them.

Accepting what you feel is not giving up on your child or their future. It is recognizing that the dream you had has changed shape… but it has not disappeared.

It is beginning to make peace with a reality different from the one you imagined.
Learning to see from another angle.
Building from a new place that you are still learning to inhabit.

With time—and yes, time is a quiet ally—the heart stops running and begins to walk.
Not because the path becomes easy,
but because you begin to discover your strength.

And that, even if you do not believe it today,
will come too.

Family as the First Support

When a diagnosis arrives, it is not only a mother's heart that trembles—the entire home does.

The news touches everyone—the partner, the siblings, the grandparents, and those closest to you—and each person tries to make sense of that impact in their own way, with their own silences, fears, and questions.

That is why it is so important to talk, to support, and to allow yourself to be supported.
Talk to those who love you, even if your voice trembles.
Talk so you do not carry alone what feels heavy.
Talk so your home does not fill with assumptions or silences that hurt more than the truth.

Because silence does not protect; it only adds weight to places that are already tired.
And you are already carrying enough.

Allow yourself to open space for those who are ready to walk with you: your partner, if you have one; your other children, who also feel the shift in their world and have the right to know what is happening, to understand it, and to process it.

That friend who is willing to listen without rushing;
perhaps a spiritual guide, a counselor, or a therapist who can offer you calm and support on a path you are still learning how to walk.

This is not a journey to walk with those who only know how to criticize or pity.
Pity does not help; empathy does.

Pity confines you; empathy walks beside you.

And it is also important to say it honestly:
family does not always know how to stay.

Sometimes the support does not come.
Sometimes it comes halfway.
Sometimes absence hurts more than silence.

There are families that fade away out of fear, lack of understanding, or simply because they do not know how to hold what hurts.
And that is not your fault.

When that happens, it is also valid to seek support outside the expected circle.
Because family is not always just the one we are born into, but also the one that chooses to stay, to learn, and to walk with you.
Look for that support.
Look for that family, even if it is not by blood.
Find that tribe that will build the village with you.

It is also necessary to decide how you will face the reactions of others.
There will be those who say things they should not.
There will be questions that fall like stones.
There will be awkward gestures, uncomfortable silences, and misguided advice.

Not always out of bad intentions, but because they have never lived what you are living.

That is where you decide.
You decide whether to give long explanations, to smile gently, or to

simply move forward.
You do not have to justify your child's life or ask for permission to exist.

You will learn to choose your battles.
To organize your priorities.
To protect your energy.

Family—the real one, the one that stays—will be your support when the world becomes loud.
They may not do it perfectly.
They may be afraid too.
But when you choose to speak from the heart, the bonds that remain grow stronger.

And those bonds will be essential on the days when you feel like you cannot carry it all.

Because even though a diagnosis may shake the structure,
it can also reveal a deeper kind of love:
one that holds,
that learns,
and that grows with you.

Doors That Can Open

Amid the emotional impact, another reality also begins to unfold: learning to navigate systems, programs, and resources that can help your child.

This path is not walked with love alone—though love sustains far more than we can imagine.
It is also walked with tools, with information, with support, with doors that are knocked on again and again.

There are programs, supports, services, and specialists
that can make a real difference in your child's life.
Not all of them arrive at the same time
or in the same way for every family.

They are not always easy to find.
The truth is that it takes persistence,
patience, and an energy that feels impossible to access when the heart is tired.

Other times, they come from unexpected places:
a social worker who guides you,
a teacher who becomes an ally,
another mother who shares a resource you never imagined.
Ask. Knock on doors.
Knock again if necessary.

Information is power, and every piece of it can become an opportunity for your child.
You will not always receive immediate answers.
Sometimes there will be silence.
Sometimes bureaucracy. Sometimes misunderstanding.

But every attempt opens a path, even if you do not see it in the moment.
Every form submitted, every appointment scheduled, every difficult conversation
builds a bridge toward something better.

And in the middle of that process—of looking outward, of knocking on doors, of gathering information—there is something you can also begin to build at home: routines.

Routines are not rigidity; they are an embrace.
They give your child solid ground when the world feels too unpredictable.

They provide structure, order, anticipation.
They help them understand what comes next,
and that, many times, reduces anxiety more than we imagine.

This is not about perfect schedules or flawlessly organized days.
It is about small anchors that help steady what sometimes feels like a storm.

A morning routine.
A sense of order at mealtimes.
A predictable way to end the day.
Small gestures that, when repeated consistently,
build a sense of security.

Because in a world that changed suddenly,
everything that offers stability becomes a form of care.
This path requires external resources, of course…
but also structure.

And little by little, you will learn to build both.

Learning the New Language and Reclaiming Your Voice

When a diagnosis arrives, it doesn't just change your life:
it also changes the language of the world around you.

The world of disability has its own language.
Suddenly, acronyms you've never heard before appear, evaluations full of technical terms, reports that seem written on another planet. There are meetings where everyone speaks quickly and confidently, as if you were the only one who doesn't understand what's happening.

And yes—at first, it feels like a foreign language.
Cold. Clinical. Overwhelming.

But you are not required to master it right away.
Learning takes time.
Asking questions is part of the process.

Writing everything down is not an exaggeration—it is survival. Keeping a notebook, a folder, or even an app on your phone doesn't make you obsessive; it makes you an informed, present, committed mother.

Organized information will help you think clearly when emotions mix and exhaustion sets in.

Every new term you understand,
every acronym you decode,
every right you discover,
becomes a tool for your journey.

Not to win arguments,
but to avoid getting lost in systems that often seem designed to confuse, exhaust, or discourage.

And here is something essential you need to remember, over and over again:

Do not let titles or professionals make you feel small.

The system may know about protocols, diagnoses, scales, and strategies…
but you know your child.

You know how they smile when something excites them.
You know what calms them, what overwhelms them, what scares them, what dysregulates them.
You recognize their effort even when others only see difficulties.
You have been there when no one else was.

Specialists bring knowledge.
You bring history, intuition, and a love that cannot be contained in any report.
And in this world—no matter how technical it may seem—
that combination is powerful.

Reclaiming your voice does not mean raising it,
but allowing your presence to carry weight.

It means saying, without guilt:
—"I don't understand this. Could you please explain it again?"
—"What is the reasoning behind this recommendation?"
—"What other options are available?"
—"I need a moment to process this."

It means asking for time.
Asking for clarity.
Asking for respect.

Ask questions. All the ones you need.
Write down your doubts before every appointment.
Carry with you the certainty that you are not there as a guest, but as the person who knows and loves that child the most.

Your voice matters.
Your voice supports.
Your voice opens the way.

And remember this—even on the days when the system feels heavier than you:

You are not asking for favors.
You are defending rights.
You are not exaggerating.
You are caring.

Learning this new language does not take away your humanity.
Reclaiming your voice does not make you difficult.
It makes you a mother. Present. Aware.

And stronger each day in a path you are still learning to walk.

Remembering What Truly Matters

On this path—so full of new words, paperwork, appointments, and decisions that weigh more than we ever say—one of the greatest blessings is finding other mothers like you.

Mothers who don't need every detail explained to understand you.
Mothers who have felt, in their own bodies, that exhaustion that cannot be put into words.
Mothers who have celebrated a small step forward as if it were a miracle. Mothers who, like you, have cried in silence and still find a way to rise again the next day.

They embrace you without questions, listen without judgment,
walk beside you without expecting anything in return,
and remind you—with their very presence—that you are not alone.

Researcher John O'Brien, a pioneer in the work of inclusion and community, has pointed out that people flourish when they find a place where they belong and are valued.
Something similar happens with the families who walk alongside them: when they find a place to belong, the journey no longer feels so lonely.

Because when one mother finds another who understands her story, something subtle yet powerful happens: no one carries the other's burden, but both discover that hope grows when it is shared.
And in the midst of diagnoses, therapies, evaluations, reports, and prognoses… it is easy to lose sight of what truly matters.
The mind fills with dates, medical terms, assessments, endless lists, and recommendations that change every few months.
But the heart knows a truth we must not forget:
Your child is your child. Not a label. Not a condition.

Not a paragraph written in a report.

Your child is a human being with worth, with dreams that may not yet be expressed, but that beat within them with the same strength as yours.
A human being with dignity that no one has the right to question.
A person who deserves to be loved, celebrated, and respected for who they are—beyond any diagnosis.

And you… you are not alone either.
Even when the path feels like a tunnel, there are hands willing to walk with you toward the light.
Seek that support in other mothers.
You will find them in waiting rooms, in therapy clinics, at school, maybe even in the park.

I don't say this in the abstract.
I say it from lived experience.
I found that support when someone shared a phone number with me and said:
"Call her. She has a daughter with a disability—she can help you."

That call—so simple, so human—changed my life and my daughter's.
In the middle of appointments, medications, therapies, and school meetings, I found a space where I didn't have to explain anything.
Where my daughter could be herself.
Where I could breathe without feeling watched or judged.
There, we found what truly matters: connection.
My daughter found young people to share with and enjoy life alongside. I found women who understood how I felt.
Mothers who had already walked the path I was just beginning—and who became light to help me move forward.

It was a group of families that met in a church—not for religious purposes, but in search of dignified options for their children with disabilities. That group welcomed us, embraced us, and over time, became family.

Later, that group took a name: Best Buddies Forever (BBF). There, we didn't just find activities—we found something far more valuable: community. Different young people, with different diagnoses, but with something in common that has nothing to do with labels: they are genuine, loving, empathetic, and have enormous hearts.

They take care of one another. They support one another.
They love one another. They know how to be friends.
Not all help is visible right away—but it exists.
And you carry more strength within you than you imagine.

If there is no support group in your community, create one
alongside other mothers who are searching for the same thing.
Knock on doors. Seek opportunities.

It will not be an easy path—but it is not impossible.
There are many of us with the same hopes and needs;
sometimes we just need to find each other.

Because even when a diagnosis changes the route,
the love you feel for your child
remains the force that lights every step.

And when that love meets others,
the journey—though different—no longer has to be walked alone.

Before We Continue…

This new path is not learned all at once.
It is learned by walking it.

Sometimes with fear.
Sometimes with doubt.

Often with a heart that is still trembling.

But little by little, you begin to discover something that once seemed impossible:
that there is more strength within you than you ever imagined.

You learn to live one day at a time.
To ask for help.
To understand a new language.
To knock on doors.
To find resources where you once saw only uncertainty.

And above all, you begin to remember what truly matters:

Your child is still your child.
Life has not lost its value.
Love has not changed its nature… it has simply found a different path.

This new journey does not come with a perfect map,
but it does have something that makes it easier to walk:
the ability to keep moving forward, even when you don't yet know exactly where you're going.

Every conversation, every lesson, every small step forward—no matter how small—begins to trace a path you once could not see. And in that process, you also discover something profound:
you are not only learning how to support your child…
you are also learning to know yourself again.

Because this path transforms.

It transforms the way you see, your priorities, the way you understand life and love.

What once seemed important begins to lose its weight,
and other things—simpler, more human—begin to take their place.

Even so, there is something that makes this journey more bearable than any tool or piece of information:
the people who show up to walk alongside us.

Because when fear is no longer carried alone,
and love meets others who understand your story,
the path begins to feel a little more human.

And in that companionship—sometimes quiet, sometimes filled with familiar voices—many mothers discover something that deeply changes the experience of this journey:

they do not have to carry everything on their own.

And that, too, is part of learning how to move forward.

"When a new path begins, strength appears where you least expected it."

✦

7.

Carrying Each Other Through

"Even the strongest mother needs

a place her soul can rest."

The Care We Need, Too

After reading the stories in Chapter Five—those honest, courageous, deeply human voices—it's impossible not to feel something shift inside your chest.

Each testimony leaves a mark:
a wound we recognize, a strength we admire,
a quiet hope that settles softly inside us.
And when we close that section, filled with love and truth, an inevitable question arises:

And now… what do I do with myself?

Because the stories of other mothers hold us—yes.
They remind us that we are not alone.
They show us that there is light, even along the most difficult paths.

But after reading them, we return to our own story.
Real life is still there:
the long days, the therapies, the meetings and evaluations,
the sleepless nights, the worries that never fully quiet down,
the fear, the uncertainty,
the family that also needs our attention…
and that deep exhaustion that settles into the soul.

And that's when we begin to realize something we were almost never taught:
It is not enough to fight for our children.
We also need to learn how to care for ourselves.

And I know. I know there is never enough time.
That there is always something waiting.

That thinking about ourselves feels like a luxury—
something secondary, almost impossible to imagine.

And yet—and I say this with all honesty and with my heart fully open— it is not a luxury. It is a necessity.

I came to understand this—reluctantly—one day,
while searching for resources and support for my daughter.

Someone, perhaps noticing the urgency in me,
or the exhaustion written across my face and eyes,
asked me with genuine concern and kindness:

— *"And what about you? What do you do for yourself?"*

My reaction was immediate and defensive, as if the question itself were an offense:

— *"Please don't give me the whole oxygen-mask talk. On my plane, there's only one mask, and that mask is for my daughter."*

I said it with complete conviction… and with all my love.

The silence that followed became the mirror I needed.
There was no reply, no judgment—
but I heard myself.
And what I discovered shook me.

Did I truly believe I could continue holding my daughter up without taking care of myself?
Wasn't it obvious that if I burned out, she would also lose the support she needed most?
As mothers, we often say:

"I would give my life for my child."
And yes, it's true.

But in that moment, I understood something even deeper:
Our children do not need us to die for them.
They need us to live for them.

And if we want to live for them—with presence, strength, love, and clarity— we need to care for ourselves.

We need rest.
Spaces of our own.
Pauses. Silence. Help.
Companionship. Medical care.
Emotional support.

We need to hold ourselves up, too.

And no, this is not selfishness. This is love.
Love for our children, yes… but also love for ourselves.

This chapter is meant to be exactly that:
a gentle pause after so many intense stories.

A breath.

A reminder that you matter too.
That your well-being is not optional—it is essential.
That caring for yourself does not take you away from your children…
it brings you closer to them from a healthier place.

Here, we will talk about small but powerful gestures.

Simple rituals that help us breathe again.
About asking for help without guilt,
and allowing others into our "village."

About caring for family life—including our partners and other children, who are also walking this path beside us.

We will talk about what it truly means to "put on the mask"
so we can care for those we love.

About learning to live not only for them,
but also for ourselves— and for the mothers who still have not realized that even the strongest among us need rest.

And about the profound refuge
that only another special-needs mother can offer—
because she does not need explanations to understand.

Because after listening to the voices that have accompanied us—
with their stories, their fears, and their triumphs—
now it is time to listen to our own.

To see ourselves again.
To hold ourselves.
To heal.
To keep living.

Because caring and loving does not mean losing ourselves.
And because when we hold one another up,
we discover something deeply true:

We were never meant to do this alone.

Small Rituals to Stay Connected to Myself

Caregiver burnout does not announce itself.

It settles in quietly—through sleepless nights, endless appointments, living in constant alert, and carrying decisions that never seem to wait.
And one day, almost without noticing, we stop asking ourselves how we are… because there simply isn't time.

We keep functioning, yes.
We care. We solve. We support. We show up.
And even though everything comes from love, even love begins to wear thin when it has nowhere to breathe.

For a long time, I believed that caring for myself was a luxury I could not afford.
That any moment not devoted to my children was somehow selfish.
That "putting on my oxygen mask before theirs" was almost a sin.
I repeated to myself—with conviction, almost like a shield—that they came first. Always them.

Today I know that this idea, though born from love, can also become dangerous.
Because when a mother begins to burn out, it rarely happens in dramatic ways.
It happens quietly.
It happens from within.

Not only does the body begin to pay the price through exhaustion and lack of sleep. The soul carries it too.
And mental health begins to bear the weight: anxiety, lingering sadness, compassion fatigue, irritability, difficulty concentrating, the

feeling of always living at the edge of exhaustion.
None of this is weakness.
It is the natural consequence of giving without rest.

Researcher Kristin Neff, a pioneer in the study of self-compassion, has shown that treating ourselves with the same understanding we offer to those we love is not indulgence—it is a necessary form of emotional care.

When I finally understood this truth, I realized something important: I did not need huge changes or impossible solutions.

I started with what was actually within reach.
Small gestures. Tiny moments of pause.
Simple rituals that could fit into one to five minutes of my day.
I learned to use the smallest spaces between routines.

For example, a simple grounding breath:
inhale for four, hold for four, exhale for four.
That small act helps calm the body's stress response and gives the nervous system a moment to recover.

Or drinking something warm with full attention—without multitasking—simply noticing the warmth, the aroma, the taste.
Sometimes three quiet minutes are enough to find yourself again.

Trying to go to bed a little earlier, when possible.
It does not always happen, but when it does, the body feels the difference.
Personally, returning to reading and writing has become a profound form of self-care.
Those moments I give myself, whenever I can, remind me that I am still here too. That I am still a person beyond motherhood.

And that reconnecting with myself allows me to keep giving the best of me to my children.

Something else that helps—a lot—is letting go of the impossible task of holding everything in your mind.

Do not try to remember everything.

Use a notebook, a journal, or notes on your phone.
Write down symptoms, medications, appointments, questions for doctors, therapists, or teachers.

When you write things down, you free your mind from the exhausting responsibility of carrying it all alone.
Also, find small ways to move your body.
Stretch while something cooks on the stove.
Take a short walk while your child is in therapy.

Do a simple three-minute routine at home that helps the body let go of tension.

And if you can give yourself the gift of a short walk, take it.

Ten minutes can make the difference between continuing completely drained… or returning with a little more strength.

Over time, you begin to realize that these small rituals become lighthouses in the middle of the storm.

They don't light the whole path, but they help you not lose your way.

The quiet cup of coffee.
A minute of conscious breathing.

A short walk, even if it is only around the yard.
A notebook where you write what cannot be said out loud.

These are not heroic acts.
They are necessary ones.

Caring for ourselves does not mean forgetting our children.

It means recognizing that we are part of the story too.

We cannot keep pouring from emptiness forever.
We need to replenish ourselves in order to continue giving.

Because an exhausted mother cannot offer what she no longer has.
But a mother who allows herself a moment to breathe—even a brief one—recovers patience, clarity, and strength to keep going.

That is why self-care is not a reward or a luxury.
It is a profound form of love.

A quiet act of responsibility toward ourselves…
and toward those who need us most.

Caring for ourselves does not take us away from our children.

It brings us back to them more whole, more grounded, and more present.

Caring for Those Who Walk Beside Us

Special-needs motherhood demands so much that, without realizing it, much of our energy ends up concentrated in a single place: the child with a disability. And that is understandable.

Their needs are often more visible, more urgent, more demanding. There are more appointments, more paperwork, more decisions that cannot be postponed.
And with the deep conviction that "he or she needs us more," the rest of the family slowly begins to fade into the background.

Meanwhile, those who walk beside us are still there.
Our partner, holding on as best they can.
Our other children, watching, adapting, trying to understand a reality that also shapes their lives.

Many times, they don't know how to express what they feel.
Other times, they choose silence so as not to add more weight to a family that is already carrying so much.
The relationship with our partner is often the first to feel the strain.
The accumulated exhaustion, the lack of shared time, conversations reduced to medical schedules and constant concerns—all of this gradually wears the bond down.

It is not uncommon for couples raising children with disabilities to experience distance, and sometimes even separation.
Not because of a lack of love,
but because of a physical and emotional overload that, when left unattended, eventually takes its toll.
Siblings feel it too. Sometimes they don't express it with words, but through silence, changes in behavior, or a deep need to be seen.
Not because they are competing for attention,

but because they also need to know that their place in the family remains secure, valued, and irreplaceable.

Caring for our partner and our other children does not mean taking importance away from the child with a disability.
It means understanding that the family is a living system, where every relationship matters.
A marriage that is cared for has more strength to face what lies ahead. A child who feels heard grows with greater emotional security. And all of this has a direct impact on the well-being of the child who needs the most support.

We may not be able to divide our time equally.
But we can share our presence. A quiet coffee together.
A conversation without interruptions. A short outing with one of our children. A simple message that says:
"I'm here. You matter too."
These are small gestures, but deeply meaningful.
They don't solve everything.
They don't remove the exhaustion.

But they sustain what truly matters. They sustain the bond.
They prevent distances that later hurt more.
And they remind us, in the middle of the strain, that no one in the family is walking alone.
Because caring for a child with a disability should not come at the expense of the rest of the family.

On the contrary: when we nurture the bonds—our partner, our children, the family as a whole—we strengthen the foundation where everyone grows.
And we offer our child with a disability something as valuable as any therapy: a more stable, more loving, and more human environment.

Learning to Ask for Help

For many mothers, asking for help feels almost impossible.
Not because we don't need it
—we all know how exhausting this path can be—,
but because we feel that doing so means placing a burden on others that should belong only to us.
We feel ashamed. We fear being judged.
We worry that others will think we can't handle our responsibility.

We tell ourselves that we should be able to do it all.
That no one else will truly understand.
That it is easier to keep going in silence than to explain, insist, or risk being judged.

But the truth—however hard it may be to accept—
is that no mother can do this alone.
And certainly not on this path. Recognizing this is not a failure.
On the contrary, asking for help is an act of courage.

It means acknowledging our vulnerability
and allowing others to walk alongside us.
Special-needs motherhood is not an individual task.

It is too intense, too demanding,
too constant to carry without support.
Denying it does not make us stronger.
It only leaves us more exhausted, more isolated, and more fragile.
Asking for help is not giving up. It is recognizing human limits.
It is allowing someone else to hold a part of the weight—even if only a small part.
It is accepting that not everything depends solely on us.
Sometimes help does not come from where we expected.

Maybe we don't have family nearby.
Maybe our friends don't know how to support us.
Maybe our environment doesn't understand.

But support can appear in simple, quiet ways:
a neighbor who watches the siblings while we go to an appointment,
a friend who listens without giving advice,
another mother who has already walked this path and says to us,
with honesty: "I've been there too."

Asking for help does not mean we don't love our children enough.
It does not mean we lack strength.
It means recognizing that this kind of motherhood is too big to carry alone. Our children also benefit when we are able to breathe.

When we return with a little more energy.
When we feel that we are not alone.
Saying "yes" to help is, in reality, the beginning of building a village around our children.

A support community that holds both them and us.
An imperfect, diverse, and deeply human network.
People who do not replace our role, but support it.
Who do not carry things for us, but walk beside us.

Accepting help does not take away our worth—it restores it.
It does not make us less of a mother.
It makes us more aware.
Because this is not about doing everything alone,
but about enduring better—together.

And because, on this journey,
holding one another up is also a form of love.

Setting Boundaries Without Guilt

Setting boundaries is one of the most difficult lessons on this path.

Not because we don't know how to say "no,"
but because it almost always comes with guilt.

Guilt for feeling like we are failing.
Guilt for thinking we are being selfish.
Guilt for believing that, as mothers of a child with a disability, we should always be available, always giving, always enduring.

But the truth is this: without boundaries, we lose ourselves.

We lose ourselves when we accept hurtful comments "because they don't mean to offend."
When we attend gatherings that drain us, just out of obligation.
When we explain the same thing over and over, even when we no longer have the strength.
When we give more than we have, until we are left empty.

Setting boundaries is not closing our hearts.
It is protecting them.

Sometimes the boundary will be outward:
choosing not to answer certain questions,
not justifying every decision,
not exposing ourselves to looks or words that hurt us.

Other times, the boundary will be inward:
recognizing that today we simply cannot do more,
that we need to pause,
that not everything has to be solved immediately.

Saying "no" does not make us bad mothers.
It makes us more aware mothers.

Our children do not need martyrs.
They need us present—not exhausted.
They need us whole—not broken.
They need us alive—not merely surviving.

Learning to set boundaries is also a form of teaching.
Teaching—through example—that love can hurt, yes,
but it should not destroy us.
That caring also means caring for ourselves.

That no one has to disappear for someone else to exist.

There will be people who do not understand your boundaries.
Who feel uncomfortable.
Who walk away.

And yes, that hurts.

But it hurts more to live without space to breathe.

Setting boundaries without guilt is a profound act of self-love.

And self-love does not compete with a mother's love—it sustains it.

Because when you choose yourself, you are not abandoning anyone.
You are rescuing yourself.

And from there,
you can continue caring…
without ceasing to be you.

Making Peace with the Woman You Used to Be

There is a silent loss that is rarely spoken about when a diagnosis enters your life.

It is not only the loss of expectations, routines, or plans.
It is the loss—or at least the profound transformation—of the woman you used to be.

The woman who once had different priorities.
Different rhythms.
Different dreams that felt clear, attainable, natural.

The woman who did not live with her body in constant alert, who did not think about therapies, medications, appointments, protocols, or diagnoses.

The woman who, without even realizing it, moved through life with a certain lightness.

When this kind of motherhood arrives,
that woman does not disappear all at once.

She slowly begins to fall behind somewhere between hospitals, paperwork, fears, and new responsibilities.
And many times, we do not allow ourselves to truly look at that loss, because part of us feels it would be a betrayal.

As if missing who we once were meant
that we do not fully embrace who we have become.

But that is not true.

Missing the woman you used to be does not make you less of a mother.

It makes you human.

There are days when admitting it aches deeply:

it hurts to accept that parts of you were placed on hold,
that some dreams changed shape—or may never return in the way you once imagined them,
that there was a version of you who was not prepared for this path…
and who still walked it anyway.

Making peace with the woman you used to be does not mean wanting to go backward.
It means looking at her with tenderness.
Recognizing what she lost.
Honoring what she gave.
Thanking her for bringing you this far.

Because that woman did not disappear.

She transformed.

She is still alive in your ability to love.
In your intuition.
In your sensitivity.
In your quiet strength.
In your ability to endure without becoming completely hardened.

You may not be the same woman you once were.

But you are not less, either.
You are a woman shaped by life in a way you never would have chosen,
yet one you have learned to inhabit with dignity,
with courage,
and with a depth you never imagined before.

Making peace with the woman you used to be
means no longer fighting against yourself.

It means letting go of guilt for what no longer was.

It means allowing both women to coexist within you:

the woman who once dreamed…
and the woman who now carries so much.
You do not have to choose between them.
You are allowed to become whole again.

There is a silent loss that is rarely spoken about when a diagnosis arrives.

It is not only the loss of expectations, routines, or plans.
It is the loss—or at least the deep transformation—of the woman you used to be.

The woman who had different priorities.
Different rhythms.
Different dreams that once felt clear, attainable, natural.

The woman who did not live with her body in constant alert,
who did not think about therapies, medications, appointments, protocols, or diagnoses.
The woman who, without realizing it, lived with a certain lightness.

When special-needs motherhood arrives,
that woman does not disappear all at once.

She is left behind little by little,
somewhere between hospitals, forms, fears, and new responsibilities.

And many times, we do not allow ourselves to acknowledge that loss,
because it feels like a betrayal.

As if missing who we once were meant
that we do not love who we are now enough.
But that is not true.
Missing the woman you used to be does not make you less of a mother.
It makes you human.
There are days when it hurts to admit it:

it hurts to accept that parts of you were put on hold,
that some dreams changed shape or may never return as you once imagined,
that there was a version of you who was not prepared for this path… and yet still walked it.

Making peace with the woman you used to be does not mean wanting to go back.

It means looking at her with tenderness.
Recognizing what she lost.
Honoring what she gave.
Thanking her for bringing you here.
Because that woman did not disappear.

She transformed.

She is still alive in your ability to love.
In your intuition.
In your sensitivity.
In your quiet strength.
In your way of enduring without becoming completely hardened.

You may not be the same.
But you are not less, either.

You are a woman shaped by life in a way you did not choose,
but that you have learned to inhabit with dignity,
with courage,
and with a depth you never imagined before.

Making peace with the woman you used to be
means no longer fighting against yourself.
It means letting go of guilt for what no longer was.

It means allowing both women to live within you:

the woman who once dreamed…
and the woman who now carries.

You do not need to choose between one and the other.

You can become whole.

A Moment for You

Sometimes, in the midst of this journey, we forget to look with tenderness at the woman we used to be.

What do you miss about the woman you once were?
What part of her hurts to have left behind?
Which qualities of that woman are still alive within you, even if they show up differently now?

Take a few minutes.

Not to find perfect answers.
Just to look at yourself with honesty.

Write without judging yourself.
Without correcting yourself.

Just to begin—little by little—to make peace.

____

____

____

____

____

____

____

____

Before We Continue…

Caring is exhausting.
And loving deeply can be, too.
Holding others, day after day, comes at a cost—one we often pay in silence.

And yet, we rarely stop to acknowledge it.
Because we were taught that a good mother endures, holds on, keeps going…
even when her soul is asking for rest.

This chapter was not an invitation to do more,
or to do it better.
It was an invitation to look at yourself.

To recognize that, beyond being a mother, you are still a woman.
That beyond being a caregiver, you are still a person.
That beyond holding others, you also need to be held.

Here, we spoke of small rituals, not perfection.
Of asking for help without shame.
Of caring for the relationships that walk beside you.
Of setting boundaries without guilt.
Of remembering that your well-being is not a luxury: it is a necessity.

We also spoke of something deeper—and sometimes uncomfortable: the woman you used to be.
That version of you who had to transform in order to survive,
and who does not deserve to be forgotten or denied.
Because when you abandon yourself, no one wins.
And when you care for yourself, you take nothing away from

anyone. On the contrary: everyone receives the fruits of that care.

Perhaps for a long time—just like me—you believed there was only one oxygen mask, and that it wasn't for you.
That your duty was to endure, to hold on, to give everything… even to disappear, if necessary.

But the truth—however hard it may be to accept—is this:
in order to help others breathe, you first need to put it on yourself.
Because if you do not breathe,
no one else will be able to do it for you.

This is not about choosing yourself instead of your children.
It is about choosing yourself for them.

To accompany them with clarity.
To hold them with a love that does not burn itself out.
To live with them… without disappearing in the process.

Allow yourself to rest without guilt.

To ask for help without justifying yourself.
To say, "This is as far as I can go today," when your body or your soul asks for it.

To turn toward yourself with the same tenderness with which you look at your children.

And to make peace—little by little—
with the woman you once were
and the woman you are today.

Because a mother who cares for herself does not abandon.
A mother who cares for herself remains.

And before we continue, remember this—
keep it somewhere you can return to read it again:

You are not failing because you need yourself.
You are not being selfish because you are listening to yourself.

You are tired…
and that, too, is part of loving.

You are alive.
You are learning.
And you are doing the best you can
with an immense love.

Breathe.
Put on the mask.

And keep going…
not from a sacrifice that erases you,
but from the life that is still beating within you.

Because your children do not need a mother who disappears out of love.
They need a mother who remains.
Who breathes.
Who cares for herself.
Who keeps walking beside them.

"A mother who cares for herself
learns to love without disappearing."

✦

To Keep Walking

This book reaches its final page, but not an ending.

Because the life that opened with a diagnosis,
with an unexpected fracture,
with a question no one knew how to answer…
does not close.

It transforms.

Throughout these pages, you have walked through silences that hurt,
wounds that are not always named,
looks that weigh more than words,
struggles that almost no one sees,
and voices that, even while trembling, learned to rise.

There has been fear, guilt, exhaustion, love stretched to its limits. And there was also that strength you may not have known you carried… until the moment you needed it.

But above all, this book has been about humanity.
Because this is not a book about diagnoses.
It is a book about people.

About mothers, fathers, caregivers, and families who face a reality they did not choose, yet decided to walk through with love, with dignity, and with the conviction that life does not end when disability enters it.

Life changes, yes.
It becomes more complex, more demanding, more uncertain.

But it can also become deeper,
more conscious, more real.

Let this remain clear:
You are not failing.
Not when you doubt.
Not when you grow tired.
Not when you cry in silence,
or when you feel you cannot keep going.

You are human.
And that, in itself, is enough.

Your child did not come into your life to teach you resignation, but presence.
Not to limit you, but to widen your way of seeing the world.
Not to ask for pity, but for respect, real opportunities,
and a rightful place in this world.

And that world—even if it is not ready yet—can learn.
Inclusion is not a favor,
nor a beautiful word reserved for speeches.
It is a collective responsibility.

It is education, willingness, empathy, and action.
It is learning to see people beyond their labels.
And at the center of all this… is you.

As a mother. As a woman. As a caregiver.

A woman who did not ask for this path,
yet embraced it with quiet courage.
A woman who holds entire systems together with tired hands.

Who learns new languages, advocates for rights,
walks alongside difficult processes, celebrates invisible victories, and
still wonders if she is doing enough.
This book wants to tell you something with absolute clarity:

You are.
And you are doing it with love.

You are not alone.
You never were.
And you never will be.

May these pages walk beside you when the road feels long.
May they remind you that your story matters,
that your voice matters,
and that your exhaustion is valid.

May they hold you when hope needs to lean on other hands.

Because walking together does not take away the weight of the journey,
but it makes it possible to keep going.

This is where the book ends.

But the companionship…
that continues.

With all my respect,
all my admiration,
and deep love.

Because life—always—goes beyond any diagnosis.

Acknowledgments

To all the mothers and fathers who shared a piece of their story with me, thank you.

This book would not exist without the courage of each of you, who opened your hearts and dared to put into words what is so often left unspoken. Some chose to share their names; others preferred to remain anonymous.

Each and every one of you has left an indelible mark here.
Thank you for your trust, your honesty, and your deep desire to walk alongside other mothers who are still carrying fear or loneliness.

Your testimonies are a guiding light for those searching for hope in the midst of uncertainty.
This book is, in large part, yours.

With special gratitude to:

Adriana Rascón

Aracely Fierro

Elizabeth Hernández

Elizabeth Robles

Elida Gallegos

Imelda Vázquez

Juan Luis Moncada

Lorena Piñon

Mariquel Cervantes

Martin Piñon

Rosario Aguilar

Your names remain here as a testament to courage and love, a sincere tribute to your generosity.

To those who chose to remain anonymous or to share their stories under a pseudonym: thank you as well. Your voice is present, even if your name is not written here.

Your stories continue to live within these pages—and in every mother who will feel held as she reads them.

Glossary

A companion to help you understand the language you encounter along the way

This glossary is not meant to turn you into an expert or overwhelm you with technical terms. Its purpose is to gently support your understanding of some of the words that appear throughout this book—whether related to diagnoses or to the emotional experiences many families face along this path.

Section I
Diagnoses and Medical Conditions

The following definitions are provided for informational purposes. Each person experiences their condition in a unique way, and no description can fully capture the depth of a human experience.

Acquired Brain Injury (ABI)
Any damage to the brain that occurs after birth and is not related to a genetic condition. It may result from infections, strokes, tumors, or other medical conditions. Effects vary depending on the area of the brain affected.

Attention-Deficit/Hyperactivity Disorder (ADHD)
A neurodevelopmental condition that can affect attention, impulse control, and activity level. It may present primarily as inattention, hyperactivity-impulsivity, or a combination of both.

Autism Spectrum Disorder (ASD)
A neurodevelopmental condition that affects communication, social interaction, and the way a person perceives and processes the world. It is called a “spectrum” because each individual has different characteristics and support needs.

Bipolar Disorder
A mental health condition characterized by significant mood changes, including episodes of depression and periods of elevated mood or energy. With proper treatment, many people live fulfilling lives.

Cerebral Palsy
A condition that affects movement, posture, and muscle tone, caused by a brain injury or developmental difference occurring before, during, or shortly after birth.

Childhood Apraxia of Speech (CAS)
A neurological condition that affects the brain's ability to plan and coordinate the movements needed for speech. It is not a lack of effort or willingness; the brain has difficulty organizing the movements required to speak.

Chromosomal Inversion
A structural change in a chromosome in which a segment of genetic material breaks and reinserts in reverse order. In some cases it has no visible effects; in others, it may be associated with developmental differences.

Congenital Heart Defect
A structural difference in the heart present at birth. Some families describe it simply as "a hole in the heart," referring to a small opening between heart chambers. Many of these conditions can be managed with medical care or surgery.

Developmental Delay
A significant delay in one or more areas of development, such as language, motor skills, social skills, or cognition.

Down Syndrome
A genetic condition caused by an extra copy of chromosome 21. It is associated with certain physical traits and a distinct pattern of development, though abilities vary widely.

Echolalia
The repetition of words or phrases previously heard, either immediately or after some time. It can be part of language development or a way of

processing and learning communication, especially in individuals with autism.

Epilepsy

A neurological condition characterized by recurrent seizures. There are different types and causes, and it typically requires specialized medical treatment.

Esophageal Atresia

A congenital condition in which the esophagus does not form properly, resulting in a gap or disconnection from the stomach. This prevents food from reaching the stomach and typically requires surgery shortly after birth.

Global Developmental Delay

Delays in multiple areas of development during early childhood. It is often used as an initial diagnosis while further evaluation is conducted.

Hypoxia

A reduction or lack of oxygen in the body's tissues. When it affects the brain—during pregnancy, birth, or shortly after—it may impact neurological development. The effects vary depending on duration and severity.

Intellectual Disability

A condition involving limitations in intellectual functioning and adaptive skills needed for daily life. Support needs vary widely from one person to another.

Meningitis

Inflammation of the membranes surrounding the brain and spinal cord. It may be caused by viruses or bacteria and requires immediate medical attention.

Meningoencephalitis
Inflammation of both the brain and its surrounding membranes, usually caused by infection. It may affect neurological functioning and require ongoing care and rehabilitation.

Microcephaly
A condition in which the head size is smaller than expected for a child's age and development. It may be associated with neurological challenges, though its impact varies.

Rare Diseases
Medical or genetic conditions that affect a small number of people. Due to their low prevalence, many families face long journeys to receive a diagnosis, find specialists, or access clear information.

Sensory Processing Disorder (SPD)
A difficulty in interpreting or responding to sensory input such as sounds, lights, textures, or movement. Some individuals may feel overstimulated, while others seek additional sensory input.

Traumatic Brain Injury (TBI)
A specific type of brain injury caused by a blow, jolt, or impact to the head. Effects can range from mild changes in attention or memory to more complex physical, cognitive, or emotional challenges.

Visual Impairment
Partial or total loss of vision that may require specific supports, adaptations, or tools to facilitate learning and daily participation.

Section II
Concepts That Help Understand the Emotional Experience

The following concepts have been developed by researchers and professionals who have studied how humans respond to adversity, caregiving, and personal transformation.

They are presented here in a simple way to support understanding of experiences reflected throughout the book.

Ambiguous Loss
A concept developed by psychologist Pauline Boss to describe a type of loss without clear closure. It may occur when a loved one is physically present but life has changed in ways that alter expectations. Many families experience this when facing diagnoses or unexpected life changes.

Compassion Fatigue
A term described by psychologist Charles Figley to refer to the emotional exhaustion that can arise from prolonged exposure to others' suffering or intense needs. It is not a sign of weakness, but a human response to deep and sustained caregiving.

Grief
A natural emotional process that arises from significant loss. While often associated with death, grief can also appear when life takes a different path than expected. In parenting, many families experience grief as they adjust expectations and dreams. This does not reflect a lack of love—it is often an expression of it.

Inclusion
A way of understanding and embracing diversity in which every person is recognized, respected, and welcomed as they are.
Inclusion goes beyond being present—it means truly belonging. In the context of disability, it involves creating spaces where differences are valued, not merely tolerated.

Resilience
Studied by researchers such as Norman Garmezy and Emmy Werner, resilience refers to the human capacity to adapt, rebuild, and move forward after difficult experiences. It does not mean the absence of

pain, but the ability to keep going and grow through adversity.

Stigma

A concept developed by sociologist Erving Goffman to describe how certain characteristics or conditions may be socially perceived as "different" or "undesirable," leading to prejudice or exclusion. In disability, stigma does not come from the person, but from how society responds to difference.

Vulnerability

Researcher Brené Brown describes vulnerability as the ability to show up authentically even in the presence of uncertainty, fear, or pain. Rather than weakness, it can become a powerful source of connection, humanity, and strength.

Section III
Organizations and Support Resources in the United States

Autism Speaks

https://www.autismspeaks.org/

Provides resources, information, and support for individuals on the autism spectrum and their families, including practical guides and tools for different life stages.

Autistic Self Advocacy Network (ASAN)

https://autisticadvocacy.org/

An organization led by autistic individuals that promotes self-advocacy, inclusion, and civil rights from a neurodiversity perspective.

CHADD (Children and Adults with Attention-Deficit/Hyperactivity Disorder)

https://chadd.org/

Offers education, resources, and support for individuals with ADHD, as well as for families and educators.

Easterseals

https://www.easterseals.com/

Provides comprehensive services for people with disabilities throughout their lifespan, including therapy, education, transition services, and employment support.

Disability Rights Network / Protection & Advocacy System

https://www.ndrn.org/

A national network that protects the civil rights of people with disabilities. Each state has a Disability Rights office offering guidance, advocacy, and legal support.

Family Voices

https://familyvoices.org/

Promotes family-centered healthcare systems, especially for children and youth with special healthcare needs.

Job Accommodation Network (JAN)

https://askjan.org/

A free service providing information about workplace accommodations, employment rights, and practical solutions for individuals with disabilities.

NAMI (National Alliance on Mental Illness)

https://www.nami.org/

A nonprofit organization that provides support, education, and resources for individuals and families living with mental health conditions such as depression, anxiety, or bipolar disorder.

National Down Syndrome Society (NDSS)

https://www.ndss.org/

A national organization dedicated to advocacy, education, and support for individuals with Down syndrome and their families.

Parent Training and Information Centers (PTI)
https://www.parentcenterhub.org/find-your-center/
A federally funded network that offers free guidance to families on special education, IEPs, and educational rights.

Vocational Rehabilitation Services (VR)
https://rsa.ed.gov/about/states
A state-based program across the U.S. that supports individuals with disabilities in preparing for employment and independent living.

Wrightslaw
https://www.wrightslaw.com/
An educational platform focused on special education law, parental rights, and school advocacy.

References

The following works have influenced some of the ideas and concepts explored throughout this book.

Boss, P. (2001). *Ambiguous loss: Learning to live with unresolved grief.* Gedisa.

Brown, B. (2016). *The power of vulnerability*. Urano.

Etmanski, A. (2020). *Reaching for community: New ways to support people with disabilities.* Atria Books.

Figley, C. R. (1995). *Compassion fatigue: Coping with secondary traumatic stress disorder in those who treat the traumatized.* Brunner/Mazel.

Frankl, V. E. (2015). *Man's search for meaning.* Herder. (Original work published 1946)

Goffman, E. (2006). *Stigma: Notes on the management of spoiled identity.* Amorrortu. (Original work published 1963)

Herman, J. L. (2004). *Trauma and recovery*. Espasa.

Naseef, R. A. (2003). *Special children, challenged parents: The struggles and rewards of raising a child with a disability*. Narcea.

O'Brien, J. (2010). *Finding a way toward everyday lives: The contribution of person-centered planning.* Inclusion Press.

Palmer, P. J. (2004). *A hidden wholeness: The journey toward an undivided life.* Jossey-Bass.

About the Author

Cruz Elena Ibarra writes from lived experience, with a voice that is close, honest, and deeply human. Not from theory or perfection, but from experiences that transform, that hurt, and that awaken.

For many years, she lent her voice to others as a radio host, becoming a bridge for other people's stories. Over time, it was the silence of her own soul—and the personal processes she experienced as a woman and as a mother—that led her to write as a way to accompany, to heal, and to give meaning to what she had lived.

Her life journey brought her into a deep encounter with motherhood, disability, and caregiving—not as abstract ideas, but as human realities that require presence, listening, and dignity. From there, her perspective became more conscious, more compassionate, and deeply committed to inclusion and respectful support.

Cruz Elena holds a master's degree in early childhood education and is a certified coach in grief processes and therapeutic writing, among other credentials. She is a speaker and workshop facilitator, accompanying individuals and families through processes of reflection, healing, and reconstruction through the written word.

Her writing is characterized by an intimate, empathetic, and deeply human tone. She does not seek to offer easy answers or universal formulas, but to open safe spaces where mothers, caregivers, and families can feel seen, understood, and accompanied.

She is the author of *Dear Juan: What the Soul Keeps Silent* and *Gratitude That Blooms: Seeds for a Fuller Life*, a book that is part of an inspiring trilogy born from the desire to accompany human processes through gratitude, forgiveness, and faith.

Beyond the Diagnosis becomes part of this journey as a work that expands the perspective on motherhood, disability, and human dignity.

In addition to writing, she leads **Hablemos**, a community centered on reflection, connection, and shared expression, where reading, writing, and feeling become acts of healing and connection.

Cruz Elena believes in the beauty of imperfection, in the power of real stories, and in the importance of supporting one another.

She writes as one who plants seeds:
with an open heart,
and the hope that something good will grow.

Other Books

Dear Juan: What the Soul Keeps Silent
Gratitude That Blooms: Seeds for a Fuller Life

Connect and Share Your Seeds

Instagram: @hablemos_teleo

Facebook: Hablemos

Email: hablemos.teleo@gmail.com

Join the Community: Hablemos

A space for meaningful words.

Reflections, emotions, and everyday life told from the heart.

Let's talk…

And perhaps we will meet there— where it hurts,

and where healing begins.

Facebook Instagram Hablemos.teleo@gmail.com

"Writing was my way of healing. Reading may become yours."

www.ingramcontent.com/pod-product-compliance
Lightning Source LLC
LaVergne TN
LVHW090600110826
845146LV00001B/197

* 9 7 9 8 9 9 9 9 7 5 2 4 9 *